Pearls
A PRACTICAL GUIDE

Pearls
A PRACTICAL GUIDE

Wendy Graham

THE CROWOOD PRESS

First published in 2021 by
The Crowood Press Ltd
Ramsbury, Marlborough
Wiltshire SN8 2HR

enquiries@crowood.com
www.crowood.com

British Library Cataloguing-in-Publication Data
A catalogue record for this book is available from the British Library.

ISBN 978 1 78500 812 2

Acknowledgements
Thanks to Stephen Goldsmith for the idea; Loïc Wiart for the Tahitian shells;
Devchand Chodhry and all at Orient; Nick Sturman GIA for technical facts;
Steve Metzler for natural pearl info; Douglas Cortez for Cortez info and introducing
me to epigenetics.

Photo credit: Steve Metzler for the photo of his pipi pearl necklace; all other
photographs by the author.

Frontispiece: Three-strand necklace of white farmed all-nacre freshwater pearls,
with matching earrings. Made to commission in emulation of the regular day-wear
pearls of Her Majesty Queen Elizabeth II. The pearls are AAA grade and have metallic
lustre. Four strands of matching pearls had to be found, of the highest quality, with
hardly any flaws and all the same intensity of lustre, base colour and overtones. Plus
two perfect and matching slightly larger pearls for the earrings.

Typeset by Jean Cussons Typesetting, Diss, Norfolk

Printed and bound in India by Parksons Graphics

CONTENTS

1   PEARL BASICS   7

2   FROM FARM TO CUSTOMER   19

3   BUYING PEARLS   29

4   DRILLING PEARLS   39

5   SELLING PEARLS   45

6   KNOTTING PEARLS   51

7   SOUTH SEA PEARLS   61

8   TAHITIAN PEARLS   69

9   AKOYA PEARLS   77

10 FRESHWATER PEARLS   83

11 OTHER PEARLS   89

INDEX   95

PEARL BASICS

General Biology

Bivalves (which include oysters and mussels – simple animals with shells in two halves) are a very early form of life on planet Earth. They first appeared in geologic time 500 million years ago in the early Cambrian era. There are now over 9,000 different species, each occupying a specialized evolutionary niche. Only a few of these produce the wonder of nature called a pearl.

Mollusca is a morphologically diverse and speciose phylum (section of the 'tree of life'), with a long and rich history dating back to the Cambrian geological period (541 to 485.4 million years ago). Molluscs in general have only a rudimentary nervous system and simple circulatory fluids. They do not have intelligence but react to various sensations such as touch and temperature as well as food.

Interestingly they can and do change sex. Spat (babies and juveniles) are equally male or female, but by maturity a majority will be male. Usually female oysters produce the best quality pearls.

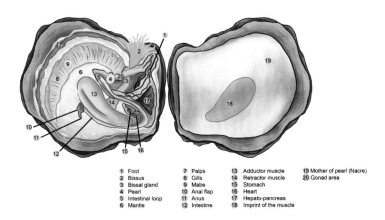

1 Foot	7 Palps	13 Adductor muscle	19 Mother of pearl (Nacre)
2 Bissus	8 Gills	14 Retractor muscle	20 Gonad area
3 Bissal gland	9 Mabe	15 Stomach	
4 Pearl	10 Anal flap	16 Heart	
5 Intestinal loop	11 Anus	17 Hepato-pancreas	
6 Mantle	12 Intestine	18 Imprint of the muscle	

Generalized diagram of a theoretical and generic bivalve mollusc.

RIGHT: **The reality – not quite so clear. In the centre is the adductor muscle, which opens and closes the shell. The mantle is the frill all around. This is a South Sea *Pinctada maxima*.**

LEFT: **A pale gold akoya pearl, as it is harvested in Vietnam. The shells in the basket in the foreground, pegged slightly open, are being assessed as mantle tissue donors for the next generation of pearls.**

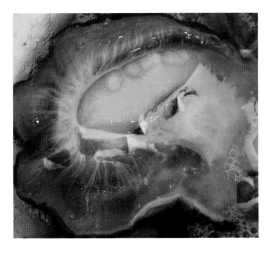

A newly opened akoya shell. Although the anatomy is not clear, you can see where some parasites have burrowed through the shell on the right and left tube-like tracks in the nacre. Also you can see how thin an akoya shell is. It is easily opened with a small sharp knife right through the shell. (South Sea shells require men with muscles and machete-sized sharp knives – and butcher-style metal chainmail mesh safety gloves.)

What Is Nacre?

Nacre is made up of 90 per cent aragonite (orthorhombic calcium carbonate crystals); 5 per cent conchiolin (an organic compound which binds the crystals together); some random organic material; and trace elements such as strontium, magnesium and sodium. Why aragonite? Because its crystalline, hexagonal structure absorbs impact damage better than amorphous calcite.

The environment adds porphyrins (which are water-soluble nitrogenous organic compounds). In shells these porphyrins combine with metals such as lead and zinc to form metaloporphyrins.

In form, nacre is made of hexagonal platelets of aragonite and conchiolin, which provide bonding. The specific lustre, iridescence and colouring of nacre — and, therefore, of any pearl that it forms — depends on the number and thickness of the various layers, as well as on whether or not the layers overlap one another.

Orient in a pearl's lustre comes from the thin-film interference and light diffraction (think oil

Female South Sea oyster to the left, male to the right.

on water) caused when light passes through the nacre of a pearl. The iridescence, or lack thereof, is caused by the size of the aragonite platelets on the surface of the pearl.

Another – extremely rare – lustre effect is water. When a pearl 'has water' it looks as if the surface is below a drop of water; it has an elusive surface translucence.

NACRE

Nacre is secreted by specialist cells of the dorsal epithelial mantle tissue.

Nacre's refractive index is 1.53 to 1.69.

A pearl's specific gravity ranges between 2.72 and 2.78.

Hardness is around 3.5 (Moh).

Classifying Pearls

There are several ways to classify pearls.

Cultured/farmed v. natural/wild

A cultured or farmed pearl is any pearl which has been produced with the intervention of man. Most pearls available today are cultured/ farmed pearls. Cultured is a jewellery trade business term for farmed. Because of confusion with man-made laboratory diamonds, the World Jewellery Confederation allowed pearls to switch to farmed as the official descriptor in late 2019.

Natural pearls are pearls produced wholly by nature with no intervention by man. Prized and very rare, until the 1930s they were the only pearls available. (Not to be confused with the description of natural-colour pearls, which are pearls that have not been colour-treated in any way.)

Seawater/freshwater

Until recently, good quality cultured pearls were always saltwater pearls. But in the last twenty years Chinese pearl farmers have gone from producing pearls that look like white Rice Krispies to large, smooth, metallically shiny round pearls that are challenging even the most valuable South Sea pearls.

Large, white, drop, bead-nucleated pearls with superb metallic lustre. Note that the camera lens is clearly visible and also that one pearl has a slightly more pronounced pink overtone than the other. Also note the big butterflies/nuts on the post. These will go some way to balancing the heavy pearls on the earlobe so the earrings sit better in wear.

Bead-nucleated/solid nacre

Until about twelve years ago nearly all sea pearls grew around an implanted bead, and nearly all freshwater pearls were solid nacre. (There were exceptions, such as freshwater coin pearls and seawater keishi, but that was the general rule.) Then one Chinese pearl company brought 'Edison' pearls to the market in around 2010. The pearls come from a *Hyriopsis* hybrid between *Hyriopsis cumingi* and *Hyriopsis schlegeli*. This development has meant that high quality bead-nucleated freshwater pearls are now available.

are on the inside of the shell, so no one or nothing will see them since a healthy shell only opens a fraction; and they don't need a colourful display to lure a mate.

Colour might be a side-effect of using aragonite to build shell. Its crystalline, hexagonal structure absorbs impact damage better than amorphous calcite. Whatever the cause, colour in pearls and their shells is certainly there and it comes from genetics (and perhaps epigenetics also) and the environment. Pearl farmers reckon any pearl is 80 per cent genetics from the mantle tissue, and 20 per cent from the host shell or environment or epigenetics.

Pearl Colour

Biologists don't know for certain why molluscs have any colour at all. Most shells live at depths that mean there is little or no light. The colours

AAA Grading System

Pearls are usually graded between A and AAA, with A being not very good at all, to AAA which

---

GRADES OF PEARLS

AAA: The best pearls. If the pearls are supposed to be round, they will be, and their surface will have very few flaws (these can be hidden in the pearl's setting). The lustre will be at the least extremely good – very close to metallic, so any reflection is very slightly blurred. Strands will appear clean to the eye when looked at from a short distance away. Any matching of pearls should be good in colour, lustre, tone, size and shape. Bead-nucleated pearls should have a good depth of nacre.

AA+: Nearly as good as AAA but perhaps slightly off-round when rolled and with a few more flaws, although these will still only be visible on close inspection. Perhaps one or two big visible flaws. Any light reflections have slightly blurred edges. Still very good matching.

AA: Average to good lustre with blurry reflections, off-round, blemishing to 20 per cent of surface. Matched pearls are reasonably well matched though there is some variation in colour, tone, lustre, shape or size. Nacre adequately thick for type if bead-nucleated.

A+: Low quality. Visibly off-round and very variable lustre. Many flaws.

A: This is the lowest jewellery-grade pearl, with low lustre and blurred reflections. Around 40 per cent blemishes, including some really big ones visible from a distance. A 'round' pearl will be egg-shaped, even from a distance. Matching fair: variations in colour, tone, lustre, shape or size.

AAAA or AAAAA: Although using an AAAA etc. descriptor is not in any way definitively wrong, it is a small red flag.

should be of the required specific shape (usually used for round pearls), smooth-surfaced (with only very small and near-invisible flaws) and of high shine or lustre. Some specialist pearl suppliers create their own top quality category to identify outstanding pearls, since the system is so subjective.

Outstanding pearls will have a mirror metallic lustre, which means they will be as reflective as well-polished gold or silver (quick test – can you see yourself waving in the reflection?), no naked-eye blemishes, a perfect shape, thick nacre, and, if appropriate, excellent matching. Bead-nucle-ated pearls should have a good depth of nacre. Such pearls are very rare in any type.

This grading system (*see* box) has two inher-ent problems. Firstly, the assessment is subjec-tive (in the eye and experience of the beholder). If the person doing the grading has never encountered really superb pearls then AA pearls will be outstanding to them. Secondly, what happens when nearly every pearl in a neck-lace strand is AAA, perhaps with really outstand-ing lustre and one or two faults, but one or two pearls have slightly deeper flaws which should really drop the necklace to AA+ but

overall it is AAA? The solution is to know the seller and read what should be a full accom-panying description. Treat the A–AAA system as a rough guide, no more, and not as an abso-lute.

To further confuse, Tahitian pearls officially have a distinct and separate system, estab-lished by GIE Perles de Tahiti and the country's Ministère de la Perliculture, which grades from A (finest) to D (poor), although many wholesal-ers and retailers now use the A–AAA system for Tahitian pearls, making life a little easier.

Pearl Shapes

Round

The perfectly round pearl is both the epitome and the aspiration for everyone in the pearl business. Round pearls – perfect rounds – are also nicknamed eight-way rollers because they will roll smoothly and in a straight line in any direction. Perfectly round pearls are at the top of the pearl price bracket.

Lovely, very lustrous, round Tahitian undrilled pearls.

Semi-round

A semi-round pearl looks round when it is made into a necklace and is being worn. A minor deviation, so that the pearl is perhaps an oblate spheroid like planet Earth rather than a perfect round, will drop the price without necessarily diminishing the appearance of a piece. Slightly off-round pearls might be more noticeable if made into earrings or a ring when they stand alone, but most eyes will see round.

Elliptical, rice

Elliptical pearls, also called rice or oval pearls, have a longer axis in one direction over the other. This means that you will get a lot more pearl for your selected size – a 8mm elliptical pearl will be 9mm or even 10mm lengthways. They are also cheaper.

Buttons

Button pearls are rounded on the face and flat or only slightly curved on their base. They come into their own as singles or pairs set into earrings or rings because they don't stand quite so proud of the body. They are a lot cheaper than rounds.

Drops and drips

Drops can be anything from nearly a teardrop to having only a slight protuberance. Drips are a pronounced teardrop shape, plump and rounded to the body, culminating in a near point at the tip. Great mostly for drop earrings.

Fireballs

Freshwater fireballs are the most common but they exist in all farmed pearl species. The bead will show a well rounded, smooth and lustrous clean head, while something has got over-excited in one part of the pearl sac and a long swirling, fluted, pleated tail has grown. The effect is a bit like a comet or meteor streaking through the sky – hence the name. Every one is unique and some are huge. They are usually used for earrings or pendants; sometimes for a necklace, but they're very heavy.

Random selection of black (dyed) freshwater large button pearls. Note the range of colours and also the huge range of shapes from shallow to really high domes.

Pastel, natural-shade freshwater drop pearls. The difference in shapes produced by nature ranges from oval to drips and drops.

Baroque

A baroque pearl is a pearl that is completely non-symmetrical in any and every axis. To the pearl farmer it's a near-fail because the value is low, but to a designer it can be an inspiration.

Nugget

A nugget pearl is one with a bit more cohesion than a baroque or a potato (see below). It often has a flat base. It can be very cheap and makes great earrings for those who want something different from the classic white and round.

A freshwater 'fireball' pearl, clearly showing the round head with the bead and the swirling long tail. (The chain is vermeil wire-wrapped tiny freshwater pearls and pink tourmaline.)

A FASHION CRAZE IN ANCIENT ROME

Ancient civilisations from India and Israel to Assyria and pharaonic Egypt all coveted and valued the pearl as a desirable gem. Pearls were acceptable gifts to Chinese royalty as early as 2300 BC, and a fragment of pearl jewellery was found in the sarcophagus of a Persian princess dating from 420 BC.

Rome fell completely in love with pearls after the Triumph procession to laud Pompey the Great's military campaigns in Asia Minor and Armenia in 61 BC: his procession included 33 crowns encrusted with pearls, a pearl-decorated shrine, and a portrait of the general made wholly of pearls.

Pearls flowed in from the Red Sea, the Persian Gulf, India, Sri Lanka and some areas of China to satisfy the new fashion craze. The pearl traders were known as *margaritarii* and soon organized into a guild. Several inscriptions have been found which place *margaritarii* trading on the Via Sacra – the most important trading street in Rome (equivalent to Bond Street in London).

One such trader was a freed slave, Gaius Atilius Euhodus. His tombstone (on the Appian Way) reads: 'Stop, oh, traveller, and behold this heap of earth on your left. There lies the remains of a good and merciful man, a lover of the poor. Gaius Ateilius Evhodus, freed man of Serrano, seller of pearls on the Via Sacra'.

The tomb marker for Gaius Atilius Euhodus.

Keishi

Keishi pearls are the wild pearls that cannot be described or sold as wild pearls because they have grown in a farmed shell. But they are wild. They grow away from the bead and have developed independently of anything done by the pearl farmer. But since it is impossible to prove provenance, the rules require that they be described as farmed.

Regular keishi pearls are usually baroque, folded, unpredictable and usually highly lustrous. They can be anything from 1mm dots in akoya pearls to even as much as 10mm in a South Sea shell. Petal keishi are very pretty and delicate-looking freshwater keishi; they are often very big – 15mm or even 20mm across and perhaps only 1mm thick – so they do indeed look like flower petals.

Sticks

Stick pearls are mostly freshwaters, and are very commonly mistakenly described as Biwa pearls (which they aren't).

Huge freshwater petal keishi, drilled through their middles and made into a necklace. The largest of these are 35mm across and perhaps 2mm wide.

Biwa

Biwa pearls are freshwater pearls from Japan. Once hugely successful, they have been killed off by pollution. The pearls looked a little bit like baby teeth.

Ripples

Ripple pearls are pearls with a folded and rippled surface (imagine the wrinkly skin on gravy or custard). They tend to be very lustrous and colourful, with patches of more satin-y lustre. They are possible in most farmed pearl types but rare except for freshwaters.

Potato

Potato pearls are the cheapest pearls. Usually in strings and often dyed, they are the mass-produced pearls that sell for a few dollars.

Coins

Coin is a generic name for any pearl that is grown into a deliberate geometric shape by the use of a shaped nucleus. Very common in freshwater pearls, they come in various shapes: flat disks, hearts, moons, suns. There are also coin South Sea hearts, which are very expensive.

Deep purple drop ripple pearls. You either love or hate the un-smooth surface.

Tokki

This term is used to describe Tahitian pearls that have little baby pearls attached to them.

Soufflé

This is the descriptor given to pearls grown by a special process whereby the solid bead nucleus is replaced by an expanding one that stretches the pearl sac and a hollow, very big pearl grows. They can be 20mm or more but are light in weight. Soufflé pearls have all but disappeared now, which is a pity because they showed outstanding lustre.

Gas pearl

Sometimes a mollusc will spontaneously produce a soufflé-like pearl all on its own, the result of something organic getting into the pearl sac and making it inflate by generating gas. They can stink horribly when drilled. Flushing the inside repeatedly with diluted bleach is supposed to help.

Tokki Tahitian pearls in all their colourful and lumpy-bumpy glory. These pearls don't take themselves seriously but have many fans for their individuality.

Pearl Care

Pearls are quite soft so do need some care to prevent scratches. Mostly it is a matter of not putting them loose and unprotected into a box with other metal or gem jewellery that could rub and damage. Be sensible and remove pearls before attempting activities that might cause harm. Other than that, an occasional wipe will generally suffice. Pearls don't mind getting wet, but the stringing silk will rot if damp – especially where moisture is trapped inside a knot or inside a drill hole. If the pearls can move between knots, it may be time to get the strand re-strung as the silk may be perishing. Clean any metal with a polishing cloth: do not use a dip or liquid, no matter what the instructions say. Pearls are porous.

PEARL TOOLS

Only a very few tools are needed:

A good pair of jewellery fine pliers – all-purpose for picking, poking and pulling.
A pair of snips or fine cutters (small electrical snips will do), or fine scissors such as cuticle or embroidery scissors.
Bamboo tweezers are invaluable for handling pearls and matching them, because when you touch a pearl the heat from your hand can create a fine mist of condensation and it becomes impossible to try to match pearls for pairs.
Pearl drill (*see* Chapter 4).
Fine needle; find a fine, long darning needle.

Also useful:

Device for measuring pearls – mechanical or electronic.
Selection of different pliers.

Bamboo tweezers.

FROM FARM TO CUSTOMER

Pearl farms tend to be situated in some of the most isolated – and most beautiful – places on the planet. A pearl farmer needs a spot with just the right stable water temperature with only a small seasonal fluctuation, and a tidal wash or other water movement which will deliver lots of plankton or algae to his hungry stock and which at the same time will sweep away the natural result of all those thousands of feeding shellfish. The water must be clean and either fresh or with just the right amount of salinity – sea pearls can be killed by a drop in salt if a river floods and dilutes their environment – with preferably no storms, hurricanes or typhoons either to damage all the lines.

There must be no industrial, human or farming run-off pollution, including animal waste or fertilizers. There must also be enough labour to work the farm. There are many pearl farms today where women outnumber men and, having being trained in what was until recently a very secretive skill – grafting – they now have an internationally transferrable skill. A farmer doesn't want too many farms in the vicinity – too much competition for food, and the environment may not be able to cope with the detritus from the shells, plus another farm may be selecting stock on different criteria.

Pearl farming is a very challenging and labour-intensive activity. In general, post-operative survival of nucleated oysters is less than 70 per cent and, of these, 30–40 per cent are likely to reject the implanted nucleus, 20 per cent will produce saleable pearls, but only 5 per cent will produce top quality gemstones.

The Pearl Farm

Raising the shells

First of all our farmer must have some stock. Farms acquire stock in several ways. They can reduce into captivity wild newborn stock, breed their own, collect wild shells large enough to be grafted immediately or buy in ready-grafted stock. Farms can place lures such as vertically suspended ropes in the water near their stock to attract the free-swimming baby molluscs – called spat – which want to find a place to settle and attach to when they are around ten days to two weeks old.

More and more pearl farms are raising their own stock in order to improve their product. They raise larvae from carefully selected parents and then nurture them with ideal conditions and plenty of food until they become spat and then small adult shells and are old enough and strong enough to go out into open water.

Collecting mature shells is dangerous for

LEFT: **An akoya farm in a beautiful spot in southern Vietnam.**

Breakfast, lunch and dinner for hungry and fast-growing baby oysters. Various algae are cultured especially for the hatchery. Everything inside the hatchery is kept very clean; baby molluscs are susceptible to all manner of ills.

The water in this tank looks clear and empty, but it is teeming with many thousands of microscopic South Sea baby oysters, being raised in an Indonesian pearl farm's own hatchery.

BELOW: The basket style used by one pearl farm – flat and with one shell per pocket. Other farms use different styles.

divers as well as being unpredictable for genetics, but at the same time a lot of the time and effort needed to raise the stock is avoided. Buy in and you are at the mercy of the competence of whoever selected and grafted your shells.

The molluscs will spend their days in open water in whatever containment the farmer decides to use – some use ropes and some put the shells in different shapes of baskets. The baskets or ropes will be linked into lines in an underwater maze, suspended on buoys.

They still need plenty of support and will be cleaned regularly (seaweeds, barnacles and other sea life living on the shells are competing for food as well as causing congestion – just like weeds in a flowerbed) and checked.

After anything from three months (1.5mm akoya on a 1.3mm bead) to two years for some South Sea and Tahitian pearls, or even longer for bead-nucleated freshwater pearls, the pearls will be harvested. Some farms will re-seed the oysters with new larger beads into the existing pearl sac, but most will take just one harvest because usually pearl quality decreases with oyster age. The best, shiniest pearls come generally from young molluscs. But there are exceptions and some oysters will produce beautiful pearls up to four times, reaching perhaps eight or even ten years old.

Record-keeping is usually meticulous as the pearl farmer tries to account for variables such as the weather and other environmental factors, as well as the choices made and levels of skill in selecting donor mantle tissue and host shells, and the skill of the operator at each stage. Donor mantle tissue is selected from pearls that are being harvested using whatever criteria the

The author selecting which harvested oysters will go on to be mantle tissue donors for the next generation of akoya pearls. First place the newly harvested pearl on the white upturned 'flowerpot', which has a 7mm hole. If the pearl drops through, the oyster hasn't laid down a thick enough depth of nacre for selection. Then assess the quality. Is the pearl lustrous and evenly coloured? If it passes, it will be used as a mantle tissue donor.

Strips of mantle tissue are cut with a special tool on these blocks.

Mantle tissue strips further divided into tiny 1mm to 2mm squares ready to be grafted. The orange colour comes from the dose of antibiotic.

farmer wants – a permutation of size, surface smoothness and lustre.

A sliver of donor mantle tissue (around 1mm square) is inserted into a host mollusc. Mantle tissue is used because that is the area of tissue that specifically secretes nacre. Its usual function is to make the mollusc's shell but it will produce nacre wherever it is – a talent utilized by the pearl farmer.

Increasingly more and more pearls are being grown around a mother-of-pearl bead, usually round; this gives a measure of control over the size and shape of the resulting pearl. The bead, with the 1mm sliver of mantle tissue, is gently and carefully inserted into the mollusc's gonad or sex organ. It seems unlikely but placing the nucleus here is most likely to promote production of a high quality pearl. That tiny 1mm sliver of tissue will grow into a pearl sac (bag of nacre-secreting tissue) within a couple of weeks, enveloping the bead and then settling down to deposit nacre on the bead.

The harvest

Harvesting is an intensive process, with all the staff concentrating on raising the molluscs from the water onto boats and bringing them back to the farm where they will be opened. Very little is wasted. Not only are the planned pearls harvested, but any incidental keishi pearls will be found either by the sensitive fingers of the harvesters or by a process which dissolves the mollusc body into a mush and deposits the tiny pearls (and keishi akoya of 1mm are routine) at the bottom of a cement-mixer-like barrel machine because they are heaviest. Shells are destined to be buttons or other mother-of-pearl applications and the adductor muscles are sold as a meaty delicacy.

At the farm the pearls will be treated only in that they will have a brief tumble wash in soapy water or salt to remove any residual goo (remember molluscs are molluscs and are very gooey).

The Pearl Factory

From the farm the pearls will go to a pearl factory, where they will be sorted and graded. Skilled staff sort pearls into strands or set the best aside to be sold as single loose pearls. Pearls for strands will be full-drilled and then threaded

A basket of fully grown akoya pearls ready to be harvested. These will be around two years old.

The only treatment at the farm is a quick wash with a very mild detergent in a tumbler drum to clean up the pearls.

onto temporary silk, with similar strands made into bunches or lots.

It is at the pearl factory that treatments, if any, will be applied. This will routinely be, at the very least, the maeshori process of heating and cooling to tighten the nacre and thereby enhance lustre by pulling together the outer layers of a pearl. The process is often likened to giving the pearl a face-lift. Pearls being treated are soaked for a time – between thirty minutes and thirty days – in a solution of hydrogen peroxide and methyl alcohol. This swells the nacre platelets, thereby closing or filling minute spaces and creating a tighter, smoother surface that reflects and refracts light better. The result is better lustre. Alternatively, or additionally, pearls can be air-dried, which also tightens the nacre.

Both these treatments, however, may not last for ever. How long they endure will depend on the severity of the treatment and the skill with which the treatments were applied (again, just like cosmetic surgery).

Coatings may be applied. They act like a varnish, again to enhance lustre, and can be a lacquer or silicone polymer. They probably won't last long. Rarely, pearls can be encased

Even tiny white akoya pearls – these are about 4mm to 5mm – are carefully and meticulously matched. Note the use of bamboo pliers. Touching the pearls with fingers warms them and they can cloud with condensation, which obstructs matching since you can't see clearly the colour or lustre until the thin bloom of condensation evaporates.

A maeshori rotary drum filled with tiny pieces of walnut shell. This is a traditional way of buffing up and cleaning pearls.

Some pearls are big and attractive but have flaws. Sometimes they have the flaw concealed with silvery coloured epoxy, which sets hard. It blends in surprisingly well. Set on the right finding and selected to conceal the flaw and filler, this big freshwater, with its pair, will make a dramatic pair of earrings.

in a thick coating that is faceted. The resulting gimmicky pearls will have the sparkle of facets but are not particularly durable.

Sometimes pearls will have a hole in them but will otherwise be so attractive that the factory attempts to conceal the huge flaw with epoxy filler. This is an obvious treatment and pearls so spackled should be accordingly priced (it's often a silvery colour, which does blend in surprisingly well).

Polishing is almost always done, to clean up the pearls after processing – drilling is a dusty process. The pearls will be tumbled with a buffing medium, which is usually crushed walnut shell (nibs of around 1mm apiece). There may be a small amount of beeswax as well.

Colour Treatments

White pearls are usually bleached pearls. White pearls are made at the factory by bleaching pearls in a solution of dilute hydrogen peroxide, often boosted by UV light. Too intense a treatment will damage the nacre and make it weak and even chalky. Even some white South Sea pearls are now bleached – good, clean, white South Sea pearls are worth more than very pale champagne ones.

International tastes for the resulting 'white' varies. Americans especially like their white akoya pearls to have a blush of pink, so a very faint rose tint is added after bleaching. In parts of Europe simple white pearls are popular, or white with a silver overtone, making a 'hard' white. In other parts of Europe and in India they like their pearls to be creamier.

Dyes

Sometimes pearls are dyed loose and sometimes when they're already made into strands. If

Pearls sitting in UV light and a very mild bleach solution to turn them white.

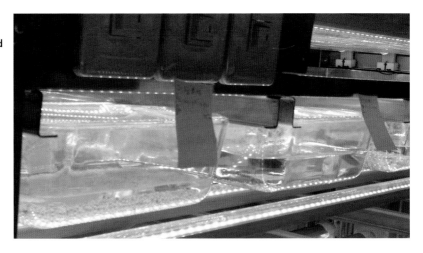

the strand's silk has zebra stripes of colour and white, then clearly it has been dyed.

Black (akoya and freshwater) pearls are always dyed. While akoya black pearls will usually be a uniform black, black-dyed freshwaters can be greenish, blueish, aubergine or brown, depending to some extent on the original colour. A black freshwater pearl which really is black has probably been over-processed.

Within the last decade the deep dye colours of freshwater pearls have all but disappeared. Ten years ago cheap strands of potato pearls of indifferent quality and colours in every possible shade were readily available, but now quality has improved and fashion has moved on, and natural and undyed pearls are the norm.

Few Tahitian pearls are dyed; the exception is chocolate-brown. There was a brief craze for chocolate-brown Tahitian pearls a few years ago and almost all of them were dyed. If a chocolate strand is well matched, suspect dye. Chocolate-brown Tahitian pearls are possible, but they are not the norm; you might see one or two in a multicoloured strand, for example.

Some pearls are being dyed so that they can be passed off as deep gold South Sea pearls. Pale champagne South Sea pearls and bead-nucleated freshwater pearls are both being dyed to imitate the deep gold of some of the most valuable pearls around. They look

convincing on their own but en masse most of these pearls have a slight brown tinge, which is a real give-away.

Once all treatments are concluded the pearls will be sized, graded and sorted, firstly into like collections and then into strands, with the very best of any lot being kept aside as single pearls, often left undrilled. After all processes the pearls might again have a quick tumble in walnut shell to remove drilling dust; then they will be ready for the next stage of their progress to jewellery.

Measuring Pearls

Pearls are always measured at 90 degrees (at right angles) to the drill hole, if there is one, or where the pearl would be drilled if it is undrilled (this does make sense usually!). Therefore for a drop pearl the measurement is the width, because it will usually be half- or full-drilled vertically downwards from the tip.

Pearls are sold by weight and have their own historic weight, the momme. One momme equals 3.75 grams. Alternatively, and more usually these days, they will be sold by the kilo – at a wholesaler there will be two prices for pearls, kilo lot or by selection. A buyer will take

A manual micrometer. You cannot measure pearls accurately with a ruler.

a random scoop of pearls from a large bagful or bunch, taking what comes, or pay more and select only those pearls that he or she wants. This is not unfair because the buyer is cherry-picking the whole package, and its total value will be diminished if the best pearls are removed.

Pearls have to be measured with accurate callipers/micrometers; there are manual and battery-powered ones available. Holding a pearl against a ruler doesn't work. It is impossible to be accurate because of the parallax of trying to measure a three-dimensional object against a two-dimensional ruler. They are measured in metric – it's easier and more accurate. When pearls are being measured en masse to be made into strands or in lots of one specific size, they are usually sieved. It is very accurate way of sorting and measuring them (and the noise made is distinctive).

When the pearls reach the wholesale office, they are ready to go out into the jewellery world. The next part of the supply chain will be a retailer buying for their own jewellery business or a wholesaler aiming to supply the market in another country. There are also several huge trade-only exhibition/fairs around the world, with the biggest being the Hong Kong shows and the annual show In Tucson, USA. Again, buyers will travel at these times to events because they know that wholesalers will have been building up their stocks to supply. The Hong Kong shows are huge; around 200–300 different pearl wholesalers sell there, with buyers from around the world (and the pearl hall is only one hall of many, with some containing precious and semi-precious gem stones, and others full of diamonds and gold and silver findings).

For total accuracy (until the batteries go flat) an electronic micrometer is ideal. It measures millimetres to two decimal places.

There is no real substitute for personally selecting every single pearl you wish to stock. With the best of intentions and business friendship, it is only realistic that if buying remotely a seller will simply take the next strand or strands in the hank and not make a selection. If you cannot travel to your supplier, find someone who can and whose expertise you trust.

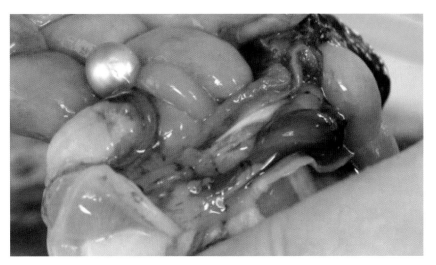

The moment when the pearl farmer finds out if his years of work have been successful – a pearl released from the oyster. Here, a gold South Sea drop pearl from a farm in Indonesia.

GLOBAL WARMING

Molluscs in all their forms are a very old form of life on earth. Their fossil record shows that species have come and gone all through the millennia. This is undoubtedly partly because molluscs are very simple forms of life. Each species fills a small and specific evolutionary and environmental niche, with a small and fixed envelope for survival. (By contrast humans can cope with a huge range of ever-changing conditions so find it easy to adapt and survive.) If one species fails in one specific place, the likelihood is that it will also be established or become established somewhere else that has those conditions. And another species will be moving in because changed conditions are perfect for species two.

Global warming is already affecting pearl farming. When water temperature rises beyond the specific mollusc's envelope, it will die. This is already happening to akoya in Vietnam: shell mortality is climbing month on month.

It's the same with salinity. When a pearl farm near a river mouth experiences a torrential storm that floods the river, it will reduce the salinity in the sea water, increase contaminated run-off and general water murk, and molluscs will die (plus there will be physical destruction of the farm lines). In times of drought, salinity will increase and, again, those sensitive molluscs will die. Acidification of the water or an increase in metals will also add to mortality.

Rising sea levels could leave some farms simply underwater – the atolls of French Polynesia could disappear altogether. Farms may have to move to find new locations where conditions are more favourable, either taking trained staff with them or abandoning skilled staff, often in isolated locations, who rely on them for their living.

BUYING PEARLS

Buying Outlets

It's relatively easy to buy pearls. You can go to a 'bricks and mortar' jewellery shop, you can look on an internet selling platform such as Amazon or eBay, you can watch a TV selling channel, go to one of the specialist pearl suppliers on the internet, purchase as a holiday souvenir or you can buy from charity shops, auctions and probably other ways too.

To put it bluntly, you pay your money and take your choice.

Jewellery shops

High street shops typically tend to carry a small stock of a couple of white round pearl necklaces and a card of different-sized white studs. They'll probably be AAA grade, but at the lower end of that grade, or AA+. These are the pearls that most people identify as pearls: small, white and round. There is nothing wrong with buying from your local jeweller, and indeed supporting a local trader is a good thing, but there are three issues with doing this:

1. The staff will probably not know much about pearls. They may well be highly qualified and knowledgeable about diamonds

and other precious stones and metals, but pearls are a different knowledge-set altogether.

2. There won't be much choice. They don't sell many pearls so don't stock many pearls.

3. They will not have sourced their stock themselves, but will be buying from national importers. This adds another tier to the supply chain, and another business that wants to make their own profit. If the pearl importer doesn't make the jewellery from the pearls they import but in turn supplies a maker, this will add to the final price.

Internet selling platforms, e.g. Amazon and eBay

Amazon tends to hold its sellers more to account than the sprawling hubbub of eBay. Do bear

An extreme example of the danger of buying remotely via an online auction site and from a generic photo. These were described as gold South Sea pearls. They're not even passable freshwaters, poor things.

LEFT: *Caveat emptor* ... can you tell the difference between the strand of real, gold South Sea pearls and the one of dyed freshwaters? One costs £4,000, the other £400.

in mind that Amazon charges close to 25 per cent in fees for jewellery – a huge mark-up that the seller will have had to include in their price calculation. The danger with eBay is that it is not regulated so anyone buying there needs to read carefully all the caveats of the 'real or fake' section below. eBay has a big second-hand market in brand-name pearls but do remember that a genuine Mikimoto clasp (or a good fake) can be put on any strand of pearls; a generic strand of pearls can be sold as Mikimoto pearls, and even the box can be sold separately.

High-end designer-makers

Designer-makers can be the source of some stunning design ideas, transforming the oddest of baroque shapes into unique creations of great beauty. However, sometimes they are carried along by their own creative process and use disappointing pearls with poor lustre because designing and making is their thing, not pearl sourcing.

Specialist pearl suppliers who travel to the Far East to find pearls will sometimes have to go through bags like this, full of single white pearls (here buttons of various sizes in 0.5mm graduations) to find pairs for their customers.

TV selling channel

Big volumes of sales mean that the seller can afford to keep margins low, but also mean that finished designs are often unadventurous/classic. The presenters have sales volume targets by the five-minute segment, so can be a little over-enthusiastic with their descriptions.

Gem shows

Alongside trade shows, strands, single pearls and pairs are likely to be available at gem shows, but are often of unknown quality.

Specialists

Specialist pearl sellers tend to travel to the Far East to deal directly with wholesalers who make up strands from loose pearl lots that they've bought at auction or even directly from pearl farms. This cuts out several stages in a pearl's journey from oyster and farm to you. They will have an interest in pearls, plus deep knowledge and experience, and will be able to supply exactly what you want. Specialist dealers stand or fall by their reputations in a narrow market and will be much more willing and able to supply exactly the right pearls for you. If buying remotely, consider the photographs. Are they clear and of the exact pearls you are going to buy, or generic? How much enhancement has been done to the photos?

Holiday souvenirs

Places such as Greenhills market in the Philippines are well known

Both these strands would be classified as AAA: clean and round. But one stands out with metallic lustre.

for selling anything and everything. But you will seldom get a great pearl deal – the sellers are extremely savvy and they know you will probably not be back that way again. Tour guides and 'helpful locals' will be on a cut of any money you spend.

Charity shops, local auctions and other local sales

Second-hand bargains are possible, but all these outlets are also checked regularly by experts looking for that forlorn Mikimoto strand.

General Considerations

Whether buying loose pearls or finished jewellery, you will need to decide how important quality is to you. Unless you simply want to throw money at a seller, getting pearls that make you happy can be something of a compromise exercise. The remarks below are general but apply mostly to round pearls.

Roundness

Especially in America, pearl-wearers value true roundness the most. To tell the roundness of a pearl, roll it around on a flat surface. A pearl that is as near to perfectly round as a natural object can be rolled smoothly in any and all directions without deviation. With a strand, roll the strand towards and away from you on a flat surface. Any un-roundness will show itself (flaws will also show up very clearly). Be aware that some suppliers will 'hide' lower standard pearls at each end of a strand – just where you hold the strand to roll or examine the pearls.

Lustre

Some can forgive a pearl for not being perfectly round or with a minor flaw or two if its lustre is metallic – that is, if the shininess of its surface resembles highly polished metal, so that you can see a reflection of yourself in it. The finest of the finest are near-mirrors. Look at the reflection of any light source in the pearls. The sharper the reflection and less blurred its edges, the better the lustre. If you are considering a strand or matched pair, look closely at the shape of any lustrous reflection; the shapes of reflections should be the same in both/all. A good pearl's lustre will often resemble a fish's eye. Matching the shape and colour of the lustre reflections is a good way of matching pairs of white round pearls, incidentally.

Colour

Looking at the 'eye' of the pearl will also tell you about the colour and overtones, as overtones tend to show up against the reflective circle of light in a pearl with good lustre. (A round circle of light does mean that the pearl's surface is round.)

Size

Size is a big factor in pricing – generally the bigger the pearl, the dearer it will be. Pearls are three-dimensional so a 1mm difference in diameter means a lot more nacre all round, more time growing and more chance of a mis-shape or flaws.

Real or Fake?

There are two ways a pearl may be a fake. It may not be a pearl at all, or it may be one kind of pearl attempting to pass off as a more valuable kind of pearl. The list below is not exhaustive and there are exceptions to every point listed here, but cumulatively, if a pearl fails several criteria, be suspicious. If it looks too good to be true, it probably is.

Imitation pearls

- Imitation pearls feel smooth when rubbed gently against either each other or your teeth. Genuine pearls feel faintly rough – only *faintly*, not so rough that you could file down your incisors. This is, of course, counter-intuitive. Under small magnification irregularities should be visible in the real pearl's nacre.
- They will have a larger drill hole. Real pearls are mostly sold by weight, so pearl traders want them as heavy as possible and the drill hole is a compromise between as small a hole as possible and a drill bit which won't break. Most pearls are drilled to a 0.7mm hole. The size of the drill hole is not a consideration for a manufacturer of fake pearls.
- The drill hole may show the 'pearl' nacre continuing into the hole. This means that the hole was drilled into a bead, which was then dipped into the fake nacre. The nacre will not coat a real drill hole.
- Under a small lens the edges of the drill hole will look as if a hole has been drilled. The top layers of nacre may even have cracked off and be missing.
- There may be nacre dust residue on the pearl.
- Do the pearls feel cold when you first touch them? Real pearls are bad retainers of heat. Fashionable ladies of yore had their lady's maid wear their pearls before they put them on so they didn't get a cold jolt.
- Are you shopping in a marketplace likely to be rife with fakes? Where, for example, authentic means fake and genuine means real?
- Can you get your money back if the pearls turn out to be duds? In other words, do they take PayPal or (even better) plastic? (Plastic is better because to obtain a merchant account to enable card payments the trader must go through bank-account-opening vetting.)
- Does the pearl feel heavy for its mass? Real pearls and some fake pearls feel very heavy. Some fakes, with a light bead inside them, will feel light.

- When considering a piece of finished jewellery, are any findings (the metal components) right for the quality of the pearls? A strand of top quality, large, round, gold South Sea pearls is not likely to have a plated generic clasp.

- Any strand of perfectly round pearls will be expensive because perfectly round pearls are rare. But perfectly round fake pearls come off the production line pop-pop-pop.

Some of these loose, undrilled, single, gold South Sea pearls are dyed and some are naturally dark, rich gold. It's fairly easy to see which is which – the dye used has a brown tinge, which shows up when the pearls are seen en masse.

- Are the pearls labelled faux, imitation, authentic? Majorica, Swarovski, Mallorca? Note that couture houses often use imitation pearls in their ready-to-wear products so they can better control quality consistency (even Chanel!).

- If there is more than one pearl under consideration, are they all totally identical (i.e. more likely they were made by a machine process) or are there discrepancies? Real pearls may be perfectly matched (much more expensive) but there are very many different shades of white.

- Be wary if the seller tries to set fire to the item.

- Is a necklace of pearls knotted and is there French wire?

Personating pearls

Alternatively, is it a real pearl impersonating a different and more valuable real pearl?

- Is the pearl too cheap? A South Sea, Tahitian or akoya pearl grows one to a shell and it takes from one to six years to produce it. That means the farm has to be fully staffed

for all that time and the shells have to be looked after, cleaned and cosseted; and they have to survive and thrive. If the price is too good to be true, beware.

- Is there any evidence that these are freshwater pearls dyed in order to impersonate South Sea or Tahitian pearls? Look for any pooling of the dye into the drill holes or flaws. What colour is the temporary strand silk? If it's not white, it's possible the strand was made up and then dyed. Pale champagne-coloured South Sea and Edison pearls can be dyed to imitate deep gold, more valuable South Sea pearls. Pearl dealers see the hundreds of strands sold by the Edison pearl company; they don't pass them off but further down the supply chain...

- Are the pearls described as 'Tahitian black pearls'? This means that the seller has found a way around the selling rules and has used a dye called Tahitian black on freshwater pearls.

- Does the deep gold of the gold South Sea pearls have a faint tinge of brown? Most freshwater pearls dyed to look like South Sea pearls have this tinge. They haven't got the dye quite right yet.

- Are you shopping in a marketplace rife with pearls likely to be authentic rather than genuine? Possibly on the internet, or at a retail outlet in a holiday resort or location?
- Are the pearls graded as anything other than A–AAA, with perhaps a good explanation of any special company designation for outstanding quality? Are medium-grade pearls being talked-up as something more valuable and desirable?
- Does the seller have a good reputation, can they respond quickly and accurately to enquiries? How do they deal with complaints? How about returns? Have they been in business for some time?
- When considering a piece of finished jewel-lery, are any findings (the metal components) right for the quality of the pearls? A strand of top quality, large, round, gold South Sea pearls is not likely to have a plated generic clasp. It's possible but not probable.
- Can you see a bead when you roll a strand of pearls on a flat surface? If the nacre flashes at you – known as blinking – you have a strand of pearls which has been harvested much too quickly, or else something went wrong during growing, or the oyster died but the half-grown pearl was retrieved by the farmer. This results in too thin a layer of nacre over the nucleus. This is especially true of akoya pearls.

MIKIMOTO

Born in 1858 in Toba on Japan's Shima peninsula, Kokichi Mikimoto was the eldest son of a noodle-shop owner, later expanding to supply charcoal and vegetables. Mikimoto became interested in the valuable natural pearls that were collected by local Ama girls deepdiving the increasingly depleted stocks. By the age of 20 he was starting to work on culturing pearls by selecting akoya pearls and in 1893 his wife, Ume, pulled a basket of akoya oysters from the sea and found a mabé-type half-round pearl in one. His first patent came in 1896 and he located the fledgeling business on Ojima Island, which was renamed Pearl Island.

Mikimoto did not know that government biologist Tokichi Nishikawa and a carpenter, Tatsuhei Mise, had each spent time in Australia and learned the secret to spherical pearl production from expatriate British marine biologist William Saville-Kent — that inserting a piece of mantle tissue with a nucleus into an oyster's body creates a pearl sack. Mise received a 1907 patent for this grafting needle. When Nishikawa applied in the same year, he realized that Mise had already secured a patent. They decided to work together and renamed their process the Mise-Nishikawa method.

Mikimoto had received a patent in 1896 for producing hemispherical pearls, or mabés, and a 1908 patent for culturing in mantle tissue, but he could not use the Mise-Nishikawa method without invalidating his own patents. Mikimoto then altered his patent application to cover a technique to make round pearls in mantle tissue, which was granted in 1916. However, this method was not commercially viable. Mikimoto finally made arrangements to use Nishikawa's methods after 1916, and Mikimoto's business began to expand rapidly.

Commerically viable harvests started in the mid-1920s.

It is arguable that Mikimoto was not the father of pearl farming, but he was the business-minded entrepreneur who took the new-fangled cultured pearls to a pearl-hungry world and changed pearl-ing for ever.

- If you are relying on a clasp branding, this can easily be faked. There are probably at least three times as many Mikimoto clasps out there as there are real Mikimoto necklaces.

Buying Remotely

Buying from a specialist with a website or TV selling channel is a great way to buy pearls – as long as you find the right seller. How do you tell a good and reputable remote seller from a not-so-great one?

- Does the seller have a good reputation on the net?
- Does the seller put their reputation to stress testing by signing up with an independent audit site like Trustpilot, Better Business Bureau, or Feefo, for example? Do they display the Hallmarking Act notice if in the UK (as required by UK law)? Do they give a full postal return address as required by EU law?
- Do they conform to EU law, in particular the Consumer Contracts Regulations, in force since June 2014? (The Distance Selling Regulations no longer apply.)
- EU/UK law requires that a website selling items must give a 'snail mail' address – not an email form, a phone number or an accommodation address.
- Does the website accept plastic directly? PayPal is much easier to sign up to, with very little vetting.

Wholesalers

You may be a business and therefore able to access wholesalers. There are different ways to build your stock from wholesale. You can attend jewellery trade fairs, which are held regularly around the world and are enormous events; a newcomer can easily be dazzled and overwhelmed by everything on offer. Or you can visit wholesale offices, a calmer and less pressurized experience.

Either way, you'll be working through lots of pearl. Pearls are presented for sale by wholesalers as lots. A lot may be three or four or twenty strands of similar full-drilled pearls bound together into a single bunch of strands, or a tub or bag of half-drilled or undrilled pearls. There are two ways these lots are priced and sold:

Selection

If buying by selection the price is higher, because the person buying their selection is able to cherry-pick the best pearls (presumably) from a lot. The overall value of the lot is diminished for the wholesaler but the customer gets exactly the pearls of the required quality and quantity.

The view down one aisle in the pearl hall at the September 2019 Hong Kong Gem Fair. There are twenty to forty sellers in one aisle and ten aisles. That's a lot of pearls. (Nine other exhibition halls are filled with gemstones from diamonds downwards, as well as findings and tools; and another exhibition centre the same size contains finished jewellery.)

Kilo weight

Buying by weight means taking a whole lot if it is a bunch of strands or a whole bag or tub of undrilled or half-drilled pearls; or it means purchasing a kilo of a larger lot with no selection, or, for single pearls, a simple 'blind' scoop from a lot. Buying by kilo weight can be a lot cheaper than buying by selection (although not always – if the lot is uniformly very good quality, it will make very little difference).

Undrilled

While it may be thought that undrilled pearls would be cheaper than half- or full-drilled pearls, generally they aren't. This is at least partly because they are the exception to the vast majority of the production coming from each pearl factory. Also undrilled pearls tend to be either top quality pearls set aside or pearls which defy categorization because they are peculiar and outside the norm in some way – so an unusual baroque pearl will be left undrilled simply because it is difficult to make a final decision on how it will be marketed to a customer.

Undrilled pearls are measured – rather imprecisely – using someone's best guess as to where the drill hole would be placed if they were drilled.

Half-drilled

Half-drilled pearls also tend to be of high quality – often round or buttons destined to be paired and sold for earrings. They can be bought ready-paired, often attached to a card, where the matching is only as good as the skilled eye of the person doing the matching – or you can do the selecting yourself. Half-drilled pearls are measured at right angles to the drill hole.

Strands

The vast majority of pearls sold are made into strands either at the pearl factory or at a wholesaler's office. Strands will be strung temporarily on several threads of silk. Full-drilled pearls are usually destined for necklaces and bracelets, or they can be used for drop earrings when a single strand will make many pairs. Full-drilled pearls are also measured at a right angle to the drill hole. Always let the wholesale staff pull selected strands out of the binding. The temporary silk can break on the wrong side of the knot if the hank is bound too tightly, and the resulting spray of pearls can be spectacular!

The best way to sort through strands is to lay the bunch out with the bound top to your left. Work through them, one by one, scrutinizing each for lustre, colour matching, flaws (some sellers tuck a few poor pearls at each end, just where you'll be holding the strand – tsk) and shape. Roll the strand back and forth to see if it is round and how many flaws there are – they will show up remarkably easily.

Single pearls are easy to select – you can simply pick out what you want. For making pairs – and this process is often compulsive for

Pick a strand, any strand. Bags and bags of thousands of strands of white and natural-colour freshwater pearl strands line up on the floor in one wholesale office in Hong Kong.

real pearl addicts who cannot stop themselves from doing it – select your contenders first, then see if any of them will match up. It's not unknown to go through 1,000 pearls, pick out twenty contenders and find one satisfactory pair from that.

Note that often the lighting in wholesale offices or at jewellery shows is too bright to see the pearls clearly. Shade them with a sheet of paper or length of muslin-like cloth, or simply put the pearls in a thin-walled plastic water cup.

Buying by kilo weight means buying a whole lot or bundle of pearls. Here the lot was twenty-five strands of 5mm to 5.5mm lavender/pink elliptical pearls. Looking at the strands, some have bigger pearls than others and some are slim, while others more rounded. Colours range from a pale baby pink through to close to lavender, but generally this is a pretty evenly assembled lot, with all the pearls quite similar.

When buying by selection, one way to work through them is to lay the lot down, bound top to your left, then work through the bundle, scrutinizing each strand one at a time. Then flip the strand over to the left out of the way. Put a knot into the strands that you want. Here the wholesaler (sitting opposite me) is counting and working out the costs of each size of strand (white, all-nacre, round, AAA metallics).

Matching up natural white drops. To bottom left you can see the initial selection; then one by one the preferred pearls go onto the left side of the card (the cards are cardboard with holes punched and non-tack sticky tape on the back so the pearls stick in place). The trick is to fill up the right-hand side. You will find a photo of one pair from this huge box of pearls in Chapter 4.

The completed card-plus-two pairs from the big container. If you study the cards you can see that all the criteria were in play – size, shape, colour (including overtone) and lustre.

DRILLING PEARLS

How to Drill

Usually pearls are drilled as part of the process of setting them. You may come across all manner of claims that pearls can be drilled with a pendant drill such as a Dremel (you'll never drill straight); that they should be held under water (completely unnecessary and potentially lethal); that you can hold them with a special vice; that you can use a burr or a reamer or a jewellery saw. None of these methods is viable.

As with all things, the right tools for the job are the right tools for the job. If you want to drill pearls, get a pearl drill.

Basic drills

You can buy basic entry-level drills in the UK for about £100 or direct from China for around £50. Low-end pearl drills have a single fixed chuck and the pearl is held in two cups; first one then the other side is drilled for a full drill by turning the pearl through180 degrees.

LEFT: **Drilling a large, grey, round Tahitian pearl. You can see clearly how small the bit is in relation to the pearl.**

RIGHT: **A lovely bead-nucleated lilac pearl being full-drilled on a two-bit machine. The two bits move into the pearl through the cup/clamps.**

Professional drills

Higher end/professional-level drills have two drills, which simultaneously drill the pearl. The two bits meet in the middle (although not always exactly, which is why sometimes there is a small burr that catches the needle when knotting).

A single-bit pearl drill. The drill is fixed; the white pearl is held in two metal cups and slides onto the bit.

It's vital that the two drill bits line up exactly and just touch, otherwise the hole will not be drilled properly.

This pearl's drill hole does not line up precisely. There is an angle/step, and a stringing needle could easily catch. If you suspect this and you cannot get your needle through such a pearl, the remedy is to re-drill to remove the burr.

ened. For only occasional drilling a simple twist bit works as well as any other. The most important thing is that the bit must be really sharp. A blunt bit will overheat and burn or crack the pearl. Any bit can go blunt after drilling only one pearl.

Bits snap very easily. There's a lot of torque pressure on a bit, which is perhaps only 0.7mm in diameter and spinning very fast (up to 8krpm/16krpm for professional drills), so if the bit is not perfectly straight in the chuck it will break. Check by tightening the chuck and then rotating it while lining the tip of the bit up visually against something in the distance with one eye (close the other). If the tip stays in one place, it's straight; a bit inserted askew will wobble.

Pearl factory level

Pearl drills that are in constant use have a foot control for the cups. The right hand places the pearl, the left hand slides the bits, and the drill's speed is controlled by a foot pedal.

Bits

There are various sorts of drill bits. Proper pearl drills are chisel/spade bits, which can be sharp-

Drilling

When drilling any curved surface – but especially at the sharp tip of a drop – it helps to pass a file over the target area a couple of times to give the point of the bit something flat to bite into. With a very glossy pearl and a sharp angle of attack, the bit can very easily skid or deviate. When that happens it will probably break; drill bits don't bend. Check also that the cups are properly seated. If one cup is not fully placed into the drill body, the drilling will be asymmetrical.

It's good practice to be very gentle as you start the drilling. Rest the bit against the surface and let it just 'nibble' at first before pushing it into the pearl. If it penetrates easily, keep on pushing. But occasionally – and this is completely unpredictable – something harder lurks inside the pearl. Sometimes it is simply harder nacre; sometimes the material used for a nucleus will be hard. If the bit does not go in easily and you are sure it is not old and blunt, just dab in and out repeatedly, stopping often. This allows the pearl and bit to stay cool. If the bit gets hot, it will instantly go blunt and can even scorch the pearl.

The nacre has been punched off this akoya pearl around the drill hole because the person doing the drilling went right through the pearl in one operation rather than drilling into the pearl from each side. As the bit punched through the pearl, it took the nacre with it.

Enlarging an existing hole

If an existing drill hole has to be enlarged – the three pearls at each end of a necklace or for a larger post, for example – then by far the easiest way is by holding the pearl between your non-dominant hand's thumb and first finger and drilling through with a larger bit held in a regular DIY-type drill. If you use a pearl drill it takes some time to get both ends of the drill hole properly lined up. Marking the existing drill hole with a touch of non-permanent marker will make it much easier to line up the bit with the existing hole. If a hand-held drill is used, however, the bit will just follow the existing hole. As you become more proficient, you will learn how to avoid drilling your thumb!

It's much easier to hold the pearl and use a hand drill to enlarge an existing drill hole, or remove a burr due to bad drilling. You soon learn how not to drill your thumb!

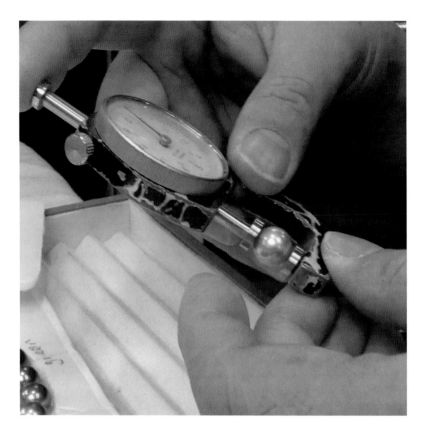

It's much more effective to assess a pearl for drilling by holding it mechanically. If you use your fingers you can miss parts of the pearl as you try to rotate it – and your fingers will cover some of the surface. A mechanical micrometer holds the pearl well.

Breakages

Any pearl has the potential to crack or split when being drilled; it is heartbreaking to see a hairline crack in a valuable or particularly beautiful pearl. It is to some extent unpredict-able, although taking drilling calmly and gently but firmly, and stopping to let the pearl cool and rest often, does seem to help. Large bead-nucleated freshwater pearls, especially fireball pearls, seem to be particularly prone to crack-ing.

Another trick for critically inspecting a pearl before drilling: fix to a handy chopstick with a lump of white-tack, after an initial scrutiny. Place where you want to drill into the white-tack and check you haven't missed a flaw (or a previous drill hole). You can see a real 'drill here' flaw on this otherwise lovely Tahitian pistachio round pearl.

This is the same pearl moved around so the flaw is buried in the white tack. Check the pearl for any other flaws and then you can remove it from the chopstick and mark the flaw as the drill spot (make sure you use water soluble ink).

Where to Drill

Judicious placement of the drill hole can 'disappear' a small flaw or allow it to be hidden under the cap of a finding.

It's perfectly usual to hold the pearl between thumb and finger to study it. Choose good light and mark the site of any flaw with a non-permanent fine marker. However, using either a mechanical micrometer or a stick and some Blu Tack allows for better examination of the pearl. Mark the spot to be drilled with a dot of non-permanent marker, then place the pearl in the appropriately sized cups and line up the tip of the bit with your dot. Check the alignment from the top and from the side by moving the very tip of the drill bit to nearly touch the pearl. Make sure the tip actually 'kisses' your marker dot. Missing the spot by just a couple of mm can mean that the pearl will set awkwardly.

Finally, and it may seem obvious, check that the pearl has not already been drilled. Sometimes half-drilled and undrilled pearls get mixed and end up paired. If you don't look at

A pair of the natural big freshwater white drops featured in Chapter 3 marked up for drilling. These have a pink/lavender tint.

all the pearl surface, it is just about possible to miss a drill hole and select a new and different place to drill...

This was an outstanding metallic dyed grey freshwater pearl. But someone wasn't paying attention when it was drilled and instead of drilling right through the white spot they drilled exactly opposite it and sadly ruined the pearl.

SETTING PEARLS

Setting Half-drilled Pearls

Most half-drilled pearls are best set onto a peg sitting in the middle of a shallow cup or flat base. The peg and cup combination is the classic way to set pearls. It's also secure. The pearl sits into the cup and the peg stops it moving or shearing off the cup while the cup stops the peg being flexed, which would lead to metal fatigue and breakage.

A quick and very easy way to make a ring cup and pin setting is to drill a 0.9mm hole in the shank and drop in a simple stud earring finding of the appropriate metal, then solder that into place. Cut off the excess from inside the shank, then make good and you have a ready-made setting. For larger cups you can shape the shank so that the cup sits into it to make the finished set pearl less proud.

Setting onto just one peg – for example, to make a ring – is really not recommended except for very small pearls. It's a style created by many designers and it looks very clean, elegant and stylish but the stress placed on the metal at the base of the peg is immense and continual minute flexing will eventually lead to a hardening of the metal; it will become brittle and the peg will snap and break.

You can see how this pearl has been set using a cup and peg stud earring finding soldered into a shank.

Multiple peg settings

Once a pearl gets bigger than around 10mm it is prudent to consider setting it onto a multiple peg setting, simply because the stress pressures are so great on the post. Making a setting with multiple pegs is not particularly difficult and need not be overly cumbersome, but the two or three pegs mean that the pearl is held very securely and cannot rock at all. The trick is to drill the pearl through the holes in the shank of the ring before soldering the pegs in.

Always finish polishing the rest of the ring to at least the tumble stage before soldering any pins; polishing around the pins simply doesn't

LEFT: **Some of the myriad precious metal findings specifically available for pearls: carat gold, sterling silver and yellow and rose gold vermeil.**

work. It does mean some making good and full polishing on the inside of a shank, but on balance doing it in two stages is the easiest way.

Glueing

Setting a pearl onto a cup and post is straightforward. First of all, check that the pearl will fit fully onto the post. If necessary, enlarge or lengthen the drill hole (pegs are not standard-

ized). Or, if the pearl is too small for this, shave a tiny 0.5mm off the peg and try again, repeating until the pearl sits properly.

Put a very small amount of glue onto the tip of the post, and then another very small amount onto the rim of the cup. Drop the pearl onto the post and to the cup. Lower and raise the pearl up and down on the post two or three

The ring with the pins soldered into place and the three holes for them properly drilled. Note that they are not in a straight line – this gives further strength. The base of the pearl has also been filed flat to allow it to make a good contact with the shank.

To ensure the pearl is drilled in the right places, drill three asymmetrically placed holes in the ring shank, then drill through these three holes in the ring into the pearl. You only need to scuff the pearl to mark it, then finish without the ring in the way.

The finished ring. The pearl sits very firmly on the shank. The pearl is a very baroque blue South Sea with applied white gold leaf, part of the Kintsugi collection.

The three pegs ready to be soldered. Note the shank has been filed flat so the pearl beds down as flush as possible.

times and spin it around in the cup (if one post only) to distribute the glue thinly and evenly. You are aiming to have a very thin smear on all touching surfaces. Glue works by creating and then maintaining a vacuum. Look closely at the outside edge of the cup and wipe away any excess glue. A piece of paper towel is ideal for this.

There are a number of different glues possible. The most commonly used are either two-part epoxy, or gel superglue (gel recommended over the more common liquid as it is more controllable). Epoxy has the reputation for being strong but it is hard to mix exactly and can take hours to set. Superglue starts to set and will hold in place within a few seconds and takes around ten minutes to fully set. (Note that it does give off a vapour so work in the open air otherwise a faint cloud will coat the pearl and finding; don't make, box and ship too quickly.) Another advantage of gel superglue is that it has its own release gel – a wonderful thing, which means that it is easy to un-set items. Un-setting epoxy is very difficult.

Always ensure the drill hole is clean – especially important if re-glueing something. Remove all the old glue.

Every so often a pearl will push itself off the finding before the glue sets, due to air trapped in the drill hole. This is an occasion where the release gel is very welcome.

A very clear example of a finding that has pushed itself out of the drill hole. Un-setting is easy and a splodge of release gel between the pearl and the cap, onto the peg, will usually easily and quickly do the job.

Ease the post and cup away from the pearl very gently. Do not twist back and forth because you will certainly break the post. If it doesn't come away willingly, it's not ready. Stop and apply more release gel.

Unglueing

Using the glue remover/dissolver gel is simple. Apply around the edges of the cup and leave for a few minutes. Very gently wiggle the finding to see if it's loose. If not, try working the tip of a needle between the pearl and the finding to loosen the suction/adhesion and then apply more gel, especially where there looks to be a gap. Keep trying the wriggle-apply process until the finding comes away easily. This may take some time but do not force it because you will just snap the pin off (if this does happen, you can remove the jammed stump with your hand-held drill).

For especially stubborn settings put the whole item with a good splodge of gel into a small plastic bag and seal (the gel dries out otherwise). Leave for a few days and then try. If not loose, re-apply and leave again. Be patient.

If the finding shows no sign of coming loose after a few hours, go to plan b and deploy the ziplock bag. It took two weeks sitting in the ziplock bag for this finding to come loose.

Setting Undrilled Pearls

It is possible to set undrilled pearls either in a cage or with claws (prongs) but, unless the pearl is something both valuable and difficult to drill successfully, it should not be done because the pearl will invariably move around and be scratched by the metal. Even if you want to make a claw setting, it is advisable to conceal a pin at the base to secure the pearl.

A very straightforward gold South Sea station necklace. The wire wrap loops are deliberately small to blend with the chain and they are carefully straightened and aligned. Loops left any-old-how look dishevelled.

Setting Full-drilled Pearls

Setting full-drilled pearls is possible – often a couple of pearls will be put onto a head pin of some sort and the other end wire-wrapped to a loop to make a simple drop earring. The four pearls hanging from the centre of the Imperial State crown are set this way. It is also possible to use a pendant cap and peg at the top of a full-drilled pearl, while concealing the bottom hole with a flat-filed sliver of silver wire glued into the hole. This small subterfuge makes such an earring look more professional.

A full-drilled pearl can also be set into a ring, for example, with two sideways-on pins standing up from the shank and pressed flush with the pearl to secure it.

Claws or prong settings

Claw settings can be used for rings, though often they are decorative and on inspection reach less than halfway up the pearl. They hold the pearl steady, therefore, but not securely. Setting tiny gemstones into the ends of the claws is an attractive refinement for the style.

Wire wrapping

The technique of wire wrapping allows pearls to be used to construct a station necklace or bracelet (called a tin cup in America). While the style demands top quality pearls, it is also an excellent way of using spare pearls. The finished work ideally has loops that are the same size as the links of the chain to blend in, and ideally the loops on both ends of each pearl should line up. It is surprising how much neater this makes the end result and how rarely it is done. The best result is if the necklace is made of lengths of chain hard-soldered onto cup and peg pendant findings, which are glued into place (align the loops).

Brooch bars

Sometimes you will come across a unique pearl, which stands on its own and can be made into a brooch. All-in-one precious metal findings are available and it is straightforward, if a bit brutal, to use a needle file of exactly the width of the finding base to cut a slot into the pearl and glue the finding into the recess.

Findings

Pearls often need specialized findings (the metal component in a piece of jewellery). The finding can be something as straightforward as a cup and peg with butterfly (nut) for a pair of stud earrings, to pendant caps set with diamonds or other precious stones, or pre-made nearly whole items which just need the pearls adding, like bangles.

Specialized findings come from specialized findings suppliers. You may have to search the web and think international to find what you want. In the UK we are used to 9 carat being the most common gold mix, but specialist suppliers in the Far East tend to sniff at 9 carat and say they don't think much of it as it doesn't contain enough gold. You may find only a few basic options in 9 carat, with a better selection possible in 14, 18 and 24 carat. Sterling silver and silver plated with yellow or rose gold (vermeil) are also widely available.

Be aware that if buying findings from America you will need to check that they comply with the EU metal content regulations for such metals as nickel (can cause allergic itching) or

Cup and peg pendant caps hard-soldered onto short chain lengths make a professional standard bracelet of blue South Sea pearls.

This crescent moon pearl is both large and unusual. It's a freshwater that's trying hard to look like a blueish South Sea pearl. Quite how it came about we can only guess!

lead (toxic). American findings can still contain nickel and it is not legal to sell them in the EU or UK. Any Americans wondering why sometimes their jewellery causes allergy problems and sometimes not, should take care to select items made that comply with EU rules.

To make the moon pearl into a brooch you need a bar finding (sterling silver full findings are available) and a needle file with a face of exactly the right size – the width of the base bar.

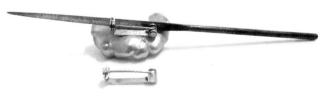

KNOTTING PEARLS

The silk thread knotted between each pearl is an indicator of quality. If there are no knots or the pearls are on beading wire and look stiff and without movement, they are not being shown at their best. It may also be that the pearls are not real cultured pearls.

The knots serve three purposes. Firstly, the chances of losing all the pearls is minimized; only one or two maximum can be lost. (Think of the scene in Agatha Christie's *A Murder is Announced*, where the pearl necklace breaks and all the pearls shower onto the floor – good for Miss Marple and the plot but very bad for pearls.) Secondly, each knot acts as a hinge, allowing the necklace or bracelet to flex. Thirdly, they prevent the individual pearls from falling into the centre of a necklace, packing closely at the front centre and leaving a length of ugly, bare stringing material at the back. If you finish an unknotted necklace tightly to obviate this, the necklace will be stiff and fixed.

It's a well-known adage that you should not get a string of pearls wet, but of course water will not damage a pearl. The silk on which they are strung will, however, stretch and finally rot and break. The silk running inside each pearl is semi-sealed inside and therefore especially

LEFT: **Nearly completed large Tahitian pearl necklace. The additional pearl seen being drilled at the beginning of Chapter 4 is now the end pearl at the foreground. A big pearl necklace like this will need one or two extra pearls, so that it is a little longer.**

vulnerable as it will take much longer to dry. If you absolutely must wear your pearls in water then a synthetic substitute can be used.

Play between the pearl and the knots is a sign that the silk has stretched and is failing: it might be time to start thinking about re-stringing. Most jewellers and the original supplier of the strand will be able to do this but, employing dexterity and perseverance, it is a useful skill to learn yourself.

Re-stringing a Necklace

Firstly assess the piece. Is the clasp secure? How dirty are the pearls? Most pearls will benefit from a quick wash in a very gentle pure soap. Put the plug into the sink's plughole (the strand might just break) and lather up your hands, then rub the strand around as if you were washing your hands with the pearls in your palms. Rinse thoroughly and pat dry with a paper towel.

Do not use any jewellery cleaner solution, no matter what the composition or claims; pearls are porous and easily damaged. A tired or dirty clasp can be revived with a jewellery polishing cloth if it is a bit dull.

Do not cut the necklace up and mix up the pearls because it means unnecessary work to have to get them back into the correct order. When you are ready to re-string, take two rulers and place them parallel upside down on a table and they will keep the pearls in the correct order and stop them escaping. Use fine sharp scissors (embroidery or cuticle scissors are ideal)

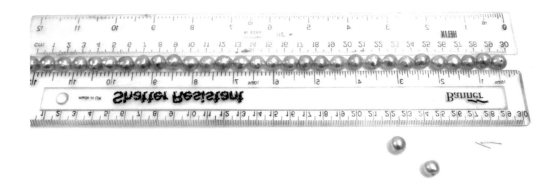

Two rulers placed parallel make a good temporary bead marshal.

to cut between each pearl and the knot. Try to cut the knot away so that the pearl comes off the silk cleanly.

Why use French wire?

French wire, also called gimp, is another indicator of quality. It is possible to use crimps or calottes, two other metal end treatments, but French wire is the proper material to use to fix the stringing thread to the clasp. The tightly wound spiral of wire slips over the silk and acts as an ablative protector over the clasp rings, protecting the silk from abrasion in wear, as well as being more neatly decorative.

French wire is available in a number of diameters and colours and platings. Usually yellow gold or silver (plated) 0.9mm diameter will suffice. Other finishes such as rose gold and

Gold French wire: one full length and some cut pieces. Note where the wire has stretched. Use this wire for yellow gold; rose gold needs a separate wire.

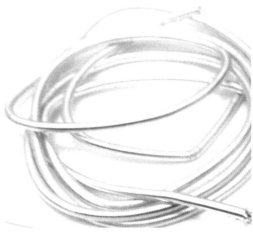

Silver French wire. Use for sterling, white gold and platinum.

There are many different colours of French wire – here is some in green, pewter and black (which would go well with oxydized silver).

colours such as black or red are available as well. It is possible to make your own by coiling very thin wire but commercial wire is so easily available that generally it isn't necessary, unless you want, for example, carat gold.

French wire has a mind and will all of its own, so cutting a new length into useable pieces immediately on first opening the delivery container is very much recommended. Use sharp snips or cuticle or embroidery scissors and cut lengths of between 0.5cm and 1cm and store in a small container. Be careful when handling the length. If given the opportunity, it will kink, distort and permanently stretch out. Different lengths of wire are needed depending on the size of the rings on the clasp. The wire should carry the silk around the rings and completely cover the silk. It should be compressed tightly enough to sit neatly but not be over-compressed, and the silk and ring should move and swivel reasonably freely. It is worth being a little more generous with the wire at the closure end of any clasp – that end will have to withstand the added strains of being held firmly, tugged and pushed.

Stringing Materials

Silk is the classic material and generally still the best. It is unrivalled for its drape (the way the necklace will sit around the neck and on the chest) and the knots will form firmly and securely. Whatever size or type of thread is used, it should form knots which will not slip into the drill holes but which are, at the same time, as unobtrusive as possible. Some knotters use fine silk thread and double the thread or more to get the correct thickness.

Synthetic silk substitutes are also available; they have the advantage of being stronger and more able to carry the weight of large, heavy pearls.

Knotting

There are as many different ways to knot pearls as there are people doing the knotting. Every single knotter will have a slightly different technique based on how they were taught and how they developed their knotting over time as they became more experienced.

Never be afraid of knotting. If it all goes horribly wrong and you have huge gaps, horrible snarls or a tangle that will not unravel, cut it apart and start again. The pearls and the clasp won't mind. French wire and silk are not expensive.

Step 1: First make sure there is a good, large and firm knot at the end of your silk. (It seems obvious but forget and all your casting-on slides right off again. Plus it needs to be firm because

First push the end pearl tight against the French wire and clasp. Dark blue silk has been used to show up clearly.

too small or insubstantial and you will again lose a pearl off the end when you tug hard to get the third pearl to sit well).

Thread the first three pearls onto the silk in order third, second and first (usually the smallest pearl, the one nearest the clasp), then thread on the length of French wire and the clasp. Slide all these to the end of the silk, stopping a couple of centimetres short of your knot. (Be careful: the French wire will take this last opportunity to unwind itself.)

Now take the needle and go back through the first pearl, easing the silk through until you pull the French wire tight, all the while keeping that 1–2cm of slack at the end.

Step 2: Make a simple overhand loop knot over the silk between the first and second pearl and pull it tight, while keeping the French wire tight around the clasp. Pulling firmly on both silk threads should do this. Then thread back through the second pearl.

Slowly ease the knot against the end pearl to hold it tight against the clasp.

Step 3: This time fasten the silk securely with a reef knot (left over right then right over left). Thread the silk back through the third pearl. Now take your flex-setting glue (gel superglue sets too hard for this job) and apply it to the two silks between the knot and the third pearl. Run the third pearl back and forth along this short length a few times to distribute, then wipe off any excess. The glue is there to hold the end hidden inside the pearl. If there is any play, this pearl can move back and forth and the loose end will 'walk' itself out of the pearl and look unpleasant even if the necklace remains secure.

Now thread on the fourth pearl and make a simple overhand knot. Slide the knot close to the third pearl, slipping your thin needle into it to keep it open, which will allow you to position it tight against the pearl (or undo it if necessary).

You now need to push the fourth pearl hard up against the third, pulling the knot tight and into place against the third pearl while simultaneously sliding the needle out of the knot. Carefully trim off the end. Position the tips of your scissors so that they are clear of the necklace, while getting the cut as close to the drill hole as possible so the end doesn't show. Be careful: cutting both threads or the wrong one is very easily done.

Coat both strands of thread lightly with glue.

Step 4: Continue to make the overhand knots and slide, push and position them with the needle and next pearl. Continue knotting pearls until you get to three from the end. Thread the

Make sure you cut the short end (we've all cut the wrong one, by the way).

three last pearls on, the second piece of French wire and the other side of the clasp (undo the clasp).

Step 5: As at the beginning, feed the silk back through the end pearl, but this time the pearls need to be in place with no slack. This may involve some manipulation to get the wire and clasp into place with the three end pearls tightly in place.

This will be your last knot. It needs to be as tight against the pearl as all the others.

Step 6: Carefully feed the needle and silk back through the end pearl and make an overhand knot. Then repeat with the next pearl. Finally feed the needle and silk back through the third pearl. It will be difficult to get the needle through because the far end of the drill hole will be against a knot which will try to block your threading needle. Ease the pearl away from the knot for long enough to get the tip of the needle through. When the silk is just

showing as a small loop, put a smear of glue on the silk so that the silk will again be held in place. Pull the silk through and carefully trim. Again, be careful to cut only the right thread.

Threading the needle back through the tightly packed pearls will be tricky, but you will find the tip will bend slightly to slide out then up the next pearl until you can grasp it. You want these three pearls to be as tight as they can be, so take your time. Sometimes you will need to spot the needle poking out of the drill hole and grasp it with fine pliers or tweezers (but do not bend the needle because that will make getting it through the other pearls nearly impossible).

After knotting the penultimate pearl, feed the needle through the final pearl (you'll have a knot to contend with as well at the other side of the pearl). Ease a tiny drop of glue onto the final centimetre of thread and continue to coat the thread as you pull it tight.

Pull the thread tight, then cut it off. Be careful to cut just the spare thread (yes, we've done that too).

The finished necklace. These are naturally blue Akoya pearls from a pearl farm in Vietnam. They are large for Akoya pearls (-8.5mm to 9mm) and have a lovely lustre. Some pearls also display a clear pink overtone as a bonus. (A video on knotting can be found at www.PearlsaPractical.guide.)

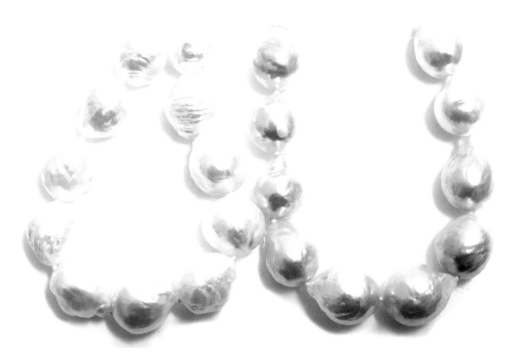

Two arrangements for drop pearls, but it is best to decide which and stick to it.

Special Pearls

Drop-shaped pearls

There are two ways to approach the assembly of a necklace with drop-shaped pearls. Either the pearls all point in the same direction or the pearls are arranged half and half, with two bases in the centre and points going towards the clasp. There's no right or wrong – it is a matter of personal preference – but it is better to choose one or the other. Pearls strung any which way will look very ragged.

Hollow pearls

Hollow pearls can be extraordinarily difficult to thread, simply because the tip of the needle cannot 'find' the exit hole. From trial and error, holding the needle vertically tip up and 'drop-ping' the pearl onto it seems to work better than holding it horizontally.

Hollow pearls can be grown deliberately, for example freshwater 'soufflé' pearls or Tahitian soufflé pearls; or accidentally when the pearl nacre has inflated on formation of the pearl sac, producing what is known as a 'gas' pearl. Gas pearls can be enormous – up to 25mm or even more. But they will always be hollow, perhaps with a nucleus rattling round inside them, and sometimes containing some very smelly organic debris.

Difficulties

Needle will only go halfway

Sometimes it can be hard to get the needle through the pearl because the drilling left a small burr in the middle: this can happen when one bit is not run through more than half the pearl to make sure the whole drill hole is smooth. Usually ensuring the needle is straight and jiggling and rotating the pearl will allow the needle to go through. If that doesn't work, a 0.7mm drill bit and a brief burst from a drill will whisk the burr away. It is possible to use a fine, abrasive bradawl but the chances of breaking it off inside the pearl and the time it takes mean that using a drill is much more practical.

Loose nukes

Sometimes you will encounter a loose nucleus. This means that the deposition of nacre has not adhered to the nucleus. It happens when the nucleus of a bead-nucleated pearl comes loose – when the nacre, for some reason, isn't stuck to it at all and the bead inside the pearl is free to rotate and move around inside. It means that the two holes on the outside of the pearl don't align with the hole as it goes through the nucleus. It is impossible to thread this pearl onto a strand without remedial action.

There are two initial indications that this has happened. Firstly, you will be able to feel and hear the nucleus rattling around inside the pearl or, secondly, the needle will only go a very short way into the pearl from both sides.

There is only one permanent way of dealing with this problem. Squirt a small amount of superglue gel into each drill hole; this should fix the loose nucleus. (If you have a very rattly small nucleus inside a 'soufflé' or 'gas' pearl then make sure you fix the nucleus onto one of the drill holes by briefly holding the pearl drill hole down to allow the glue to set with the nucleus sitting on the hole.) Usually only one or at worst two pearls on a strand are affected, but it has been known for a whole strand to have rattling nuclei.

Needle goes part-way only

If you are knotting drop-shaped pearls and the needle will only go part-way in from the pointed end, it is likely that the point is at least partly hollow and your needle is slightly bent. The needle's point is missing the hole in the nucleus or body of the pearl.

The remedy is to ensure your needle is perfectly straight and rotate the pearl. With patience the needle tip will catch the drill hole. Usually straightening with your hand will suffice but sometimes pulling hard with your pliers holding the tip is necessary.

Which silk colour?

White stringing silk is not brilliant white. It is made especially for pearls so it is a gentle white with a touch of cream – it goes well with akoya pearls – and realistically brilliant white silk would soon get slightly discoloured anyway. It is a nice touch to use matching silk for, for example, black or grey pearls. Multicoloured strands look best with a neutral shade. Or you could be adventurous and use bright red with red French wire, or green with green.

Three-strand necklaces

Triple necklaces are tricky to get to sit properly (you might notice that even the Queen has one triple strand with a slightly too-long lowest strand). One way to make such a necklace is to make and finish the middle strand first, making sure that it sits long enough that the short strand will not choke the wearer, then add the top strand, and finally the longest. Also make sure you connect the strands to the clasp in the right order. The only really satisfactory way to ensure that the three strands do sit properly is to keep trying them

A Tahitian pearl on a 2mm round leather thong. Notice how the knots on either side of the pearl are mirror images. It can take some time to work out how to do mirror knots.

on before finishing each strand, keeping around eight pearls threaded on but unknotted so that you can add or remove them as necessary.

Remember, if your first attempt at knotting goes wrong, simply take the necklace apart and try again. The pearls won't mind and all you will have lost is a short length of silk and two small pieces of French wire.

Pearls on leather

Pearls and leather are a great combination. They have a beach/surf vibe and even the most English of men will find themselves able to wear a dark, circle Tahitian pearl set onto a manly length of dark leather.

There isn't much involved in the actual assembly of such a necklace or bracelet. But the pearl itself will have to have its drill hole enlarged to allow it to be threaded onto a length of leather which may be 1mm in diameter or (quite often) up to 2mm. That does involve some determined drilling and you'll need to start with quite a big pearl.

Threading the pearl onto the leather is straightforward and the neatest way to finish the piece is to do a single overhand knot at each side of the pearl to hold it in place. It is important to do the knots so they complement each other – single overhand knots send the thong off in a clear direction. Special hollow clasps with tubes for the leather are easily available. Get the right diameter for your leather and fix with a dab of glue.

SOUTH SEA PEARLS

South Sea pearls are the most prized of cultured pearls because they are arguably the most beautiful, the rarest and the most valuable. They are farmed mostly in Australia, Indonesia and the Philippines, and range in colour from white to gold, with very rare variations that are blue, green, violet, black and pink. Most prized are the deepest gold shades and the natural whites.

Comparing quality pearl to pearl, South Sea pearls will always be among the most expensive because their production is limited to one pearl per oyster and it can take two to four years from graft to harvest to produce that pearl. With two years as the average, it is clear that there is an increasing risk of a mis-shape or flaw, and the chances of getting a perfect, round, rich gold South Sea pearl at the end of the process are relatively small.

White South Sea pearls come mostly from Australia, while the golds are now grown in the Philippines and Indonesia, although the oysters themselves often mix the colours around unpredictably. The South Seas lie between the northern coast of Australia and the southern coast of China. These waters are the native habitat of the largest farmed oyster, *Pinctada maxima*, known commonly as the gold-lipped oyster. This oyster grows a shell up to 30cm in diameter, and so it can be nucleated with a much larger bead than any other saltwater pearl oyster. The pearls it grows can be up to 20mm, although 10–12mm is probably the most common size range. Because the pearls are grown on a bead they are usually round to roundish, although wildly variable baroques and circles are possible and prized for their uniqueness.

LEFT: **A rope of deep gold South Sea pearls on a shell showing both gold and white nacre.**

RIGHT: **A remote Indonesian island pearl farm – paradise.**

Their lustre sets them apart from other pearls. While the finest and most valuable have a near-metallic reflective surface, most South Sea pearls have a gentler, more satin-like sheen. This is because the nacre contains relatively larger aragonite platelets.

The outside of the gold-lipped oyster is far less glamorous than the inside.

Glorious bands of deep gold, lighter gold and white adorn this polished South Sea shell from Indonesia.

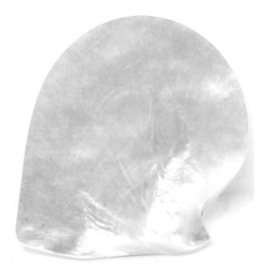

From the same pearl farm, and the same stock, an all-white South Sea shell (also the faintest blush of pink in bands).

The Farming Process

Baby oysters are either bred in a hatchery, spawn naturally and are then collected by placing various lures (such as suspended lengths of rope) in the water to attract the spats, as baby oysters are called; or they are collected as mature wild specimens, large enough to be nucleated. Spat are grown on for two or more years until they are big enough to accept a grafted bead nucleus.

If all goes well, the pearls will be ready for harvest between two and four years after nucleation, depending on growing conditions. Typically South Sea pearls have thick nacre of at least 2mm and often much more. Indeed it has recently been discovered and confirmed by the GIA that some Australian white South Sea pearls are 'super-nacrerers', producing high quality round pearls up to 19mm in 24 months – nearly 6mm of nacre or around 90 per cent nacre from a first graft.

While this results in the nacre looking lush, it also means that in those two to four years there is plenty of opportunity for something to

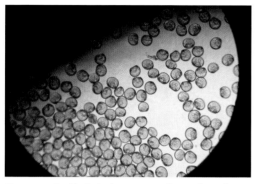

Here are the little baby oysters, just a few days old and only visible under magnification, in an Indonesian farm hatchery.

A six-month-old Indonesian South Sea shell: almost translucent, very fragile but a rainbow of colour.

go awry, from a deviation from perfectly round to marks: typically South Sea pearls have what are nicknamed 'fishbites' – small circular marks which look like a stone dropped into thick sauce. Thicker nacre deposits are valued – Philippine gold pearls usually have much thicker nacre and prices are substantially higher than for Indonesian golds.

A pearl harvest is labour-intensive. Gold-lipped oysters are big and hard to open, and farm workers have to use fearsome machete-like knives. After the bodies are removed from the shell the pearls are found by sensitive touch – both the planned pearls and the bonus extra keishi. Nothing will be wasted: the adductor muscles go off as a special food delicacy and the

shells for buttons and other mother-of-pearl applications.

Colours

South Sea pearls range in colour from white to gold, with very rare variations that are blue,

Harvesting South Sea pearls. The shells are opened with fearsomely sharp machete-like knives, which are sharpened overnight.

green, violet, black and pink. Most prized are the deepest gold shades and the natural whites. Golds can vary between a pale straw colour called 'champagne' through to the deepest gold, which is as rich as high carat gold itself. The golds can be greenish or have a pink overtone as well.

With this oyster not only is the pearl easy to feel but it is visible in the photo. You work more by feel than by sight. After finding the expected pearl (or not – some oysters simply don't have a pearl), you may feel something more – a bonus keishi pearl, usually somewhere in the mantle.

One day's production at the farm, sorted and ready to go to auction.

White South Sea pearl conchiolin is colourless to light grey or pale beige, while golden conchiolin is present in a range of darker pigments like orange, brown and reddish-brown.

Blue and green South Sea pearls are almost the rarest of South Sea colours and their cause is unglamorous – the pearl is contaminated with organic matter which colours what would have been a white pearl a shade of blue, from pale blue through to a deep denim blue. A green South Sea pearl is a gold pearl with the same

These pearls have just been harvested and then swished in some water. This shows both the variety of shapes and colours, and how rare round or even near-round pearls are. This is the result of a morning's hard work by around fifty people.

Blue South Sea pearls can be exceptionally blue, as in the pearl on the left. Often ice-white blue pearls are described as blue, when really they aren't.

Green South Sea pearl – note the blue patch.

A curiosity: a random all-black South Sea pearl.

Pink South Sea pearl. The pink shade is always very pale, but it is a body colour rather than an overtone.

organic contamination. Baby pink and black South Sea pearls sometimes appear through unpredictable unusual genetic quirks.

As with other saltwater oysters, the South Sea pearl oyster is bead-nucleated. However, the growth period is approximately two to four years, unlike akoya pearls, which develop in less than half that time. Being a delicate organism, this type of pearl oyster is particularly suscep-tible to disease and stress, which is one reason why the culturing area for South Sea pearls is quite limited. Attempts to expand South Sea pearl farming have met with little success because the oysters do not thrive outside their narrow, native, natural environment.

Shapes

South Sea pearls come in all shapes and permu-tations, but the only ones that are regularly available are the rounds, the semi-rounds and the oval/drop/baroques, including sometimes circles.

Keishi

South Sea keishi pearls can be very pretty, completely random shapes but with the stun-

South Sea keishi pearls, often the shiniest pearls of the harvest.

ning lustre which is usually found in all types of keishi. Since South Sea pearls are bead-nucleated, keishi are extra pearls and are arguably wild, although they cannot properly be described as wild pearls.

Buying South Sea Pearls

Because South Sea pearls are potentially of high value, they are also very vulnerable to fakes and frauds. Some are priced too high for the quality. Other frauds include the deliberate passing off of, usually, dyed bead-nucleated freshwater pearls as gold, round South Sea pearls.

One freshwater pearl company especially has been producing strand upon strand of good quality bead-nucleated pearls dyed 'South Sea gold'. The company itself makes no attempt to pass off the freshwaters as genuine, but with strands, even top quality ones, at a fraction of

A good example of a circle South Sea pearl, showing both white and gold nacre. It's best set by half drilling from the tip down, with a small cap to cover the askew bump on its top.

the cost, without any doubt some enter the South Sea market. En masse the strands have a slight brown tinge, but in ones and twos the pearls can be very convincing. The only way to tell without laboratory analysis is to look carefully at any suspect pearls on offer. What do the flaws look like? South Sea pearls have a distinctive 'fishbite' flaw, which freshwater pearls just do not get. It looks like the surface left when a stone is dropped into thick gravy or custard, or when a hot mud sump goes 'blurp' – a bit like a crater. Ring flaws are not themselves diagnostic because freshwater pearls also get rings.

A more subtle cheat is dying very pale gold South Sea pearls a deeper gold. Individual strands of these and dyed freshwater can look remarkably convincing, but en masse these strands all show a distinctive brownish tinge, which is never present in genuine gold South Sea pearls.

Do not be afraid to ask for more information and photographs if buying remotely. What will you receive if the photographs are generic? As with all pearls, if you are willing to accept pearls which are not perfectly round the price will drop markedly, while any slight deviation from perfect round will not be noticeable in wear. A strand of top quality, deep gold South Sea pearls should cost many thousands of GBP or USD.

Some idea of the size range possible with South Sea pearls – here from 5mm to 16mm.

A pearl farm in Indonesia. The oysters are brought to the building on the left to be opened and the pearls retrieved.

TAHITIAN PEARLS

To the east of Australia and the west of South America, in the middle of the Pacific Ocean, the seabed rises to the surface and 118 islands and coral atolls (plus over 3,000 islets) poke above the waves, some by only a few centimetres. It is here, mostly in the tiny atolls of the Tuamotu and Gambier groups, that the black pearl or Tahitian pearl has been farmed since the establishment of the first commercial pearl farm on Mahini atoll in 1966.

The black-lipped oyster, *Pinctada margaritifera*, can be found along the coasts of Peru, Baja California, Indonesia, Panama, the Red Sea, the Philippines, Micronesia and Okinawa, Japan, but it was to the warm coral atolls of French Polynesia that the pioneer pearl farmers were drawn. Here there were plenty of coastal waters of the right temperature and depth, and strong enough tides to wash in plenty of food and wash away all the detritus that goes with thousands of farmed oysters sitting in baskets.

Throughout their own local history the people of Polynesia dived for the beautiful shells, and the pearls within, found off their coastal waters and turned them into jewellery for themselves. Once the islands were 'discovered' by the rest of the world, a trade in shells for buttons and furniture inlay developed. A few pieces, which include very old natural Tahitian pearls, have sold at auction for huge sums.

Tahitian pearls are not grown on the island of Tahiti itself, although many of the big farm companies and wholesalers have offices in Papeete, the capital. The farms are often incredibly isolated. Ahé atoll, an irregular elliptical atoll, for example, has one narrow sea entrance and several tiny islets. There are just over 500 inhabitants, and several pearl farms around the inside of the atoll; if you do a Google Maps search for Ahé airport, you can see the farms – look for the piers and structures built out over the sea.

Tahitian pearls are prized for their depth of colours, their size and their variety of forms.

Colours

Tahitian shells show predominantly green, magenta and gold on the outside when the rough outer layers of shell are polished away;

LEFT: **A beautifully polished Tahitian oyster shell, draped with a necklace of multicoloured, round Tahitian pearls.**

A polished Tahitian black-lipped oyster shell, showing clearly the myriad of possible colours.

A polished Tahitian shell showing the golds as well as the greens and pink-to-aubergines in the genetic pot.

Round peacock Tahitian pearl: dark green body and aubergine eye. The dark circle in the middle of the photo is the camera's lens.

Blue Tahitian round pearl. Some sellers describe green/blue Tahitian pearls as blue, but really only unquestionably blue pearls should be called blues.

the insides are most usually white with a black edge – hence the common name, black-lipped oyster. Some shells also show gold outside, like their P. maxima cousins.

In a near-closed environment such as an atoll, farming will itself tend to fix certain colour strains and traits as the farmer selects for his preferred traits and qualities at each grafting.

Most Tahitian pearls have a green base colour. That green ranges from very dark to very light green (known as pistachio green). The elusive peacock effect presents as a disc of an extra and different colour, of varying size, covering nearly the whole pearl down to a small dot, which floats around the pearl's surface as the pearl is moved in relation to the viewer. A dark green pearl will have aubergine, while a pistachio-shaded pearl will show a delicate pink. The remarkable thing about a peacock Tahitian pearl is that this is not a fixed circle of colour: it moves around the pearl and is an optical effect caused by the interaction of white light with the nacreous layers (building on the nacre platelets' size, spacing, pattern and transparency) to produce reflection and refraction effects (resulting in in-phase and out-of-phase wavelengths). Light passes through and then is reflected by layers of aragonite and conchiolin.

Blue Tahitian pearls are not common, especially in a true clear blue. What is often described as blue is usually a sort of marine green/blue. Only sometimes the blue is a rich mid blue and other times there can be an attractive aqua blue. Rarely can a blue pearl show a peacock effect with a pink body and blue eye.

White Tahitian drop-shaped pearl: a very unusual colour.

Huge stocks of Tahitian pearl strands and loose pearls in a Hong Kong wholesaler's office.

Browns, from rich chocolate to buff and beige, are popular: there was a huge craze for chocolate Tahitians a few years ago and this sparked a flood of dyed pearls. (Dyeing Tahitian pearls is very much the exception, but it can happen.) Brown shades can go to a more metallic copper.

Grey and silver shades are common. Perhaps the rarest colour for Tahitian pearls is white (really a very, very, very pale silver).

Tahitian Pearl Farming

Economically pearl farming is very important to French Polynesia. The Tahitian pearl is French Polynesia's largest export, making up just over half the country's annual exports of more than £20m. *P. margaritifera* is also farmed in the Cook Islands and Fiji. The pearls from these islands seem to be slightly different, with localized variations in colour and sometimes a faint earthiness.

Pearls are usually sold from French Polynesia as singles, undrilled and loose in lots. A lot might be a bag of a thousand round 9mm grade AAA pearls. These are often sold by silent auction to wholesalers, who will make them

Assembling strands from loose pearls. Note the use of bamboo tweezers. Touching the pearls can cause condensation to form, which makes matching inaccurate or slow while waiting for the haze to clear.

up into strands or pairs for onward sale. Hong Kong is the main centre for this.

For pearl production from *P. margaritifera* it is generally accepted that 5 per cent of the total pearl harvest will generate around 95 per cent of farm profits. Tahitian pearl farmers usually rely for stock on wild larvae/spat lured to collectors – lines of rope dangling in the sea for the spat to fasten themselves to with their 'holdfast' foot when their shells get too heavy for them to be free-swimming. The system works for black-lipped shell stock, so most farms do not turn to in-house hatcheries for young stock.

A Tahitian nucleus is usually a round ball made from one of the wild molluscs found in the American Mississippi basin, although the demand for nucleus material is depleting and damaging wild stocks. These wild shells are not thick enough to give larger third graft nuclei and sometimes the use of *Tridacna* (giant clam) shell can be suspected (in breach of CITES). (If when drilling a very large pearl the drill bit goes through the Tahitian outer nacre easily and then almost stops, there may be *Tridacna* shell material. Giant clam shell is much harder than most nucleus material. It is just about drillable but go very slowly and stop often to allow the bit and pearl to cool down.)

Some Tahitian pearl farmers, thinking sustainably, are recycling some of their own shells to make nuclei. Farms that do this report that their harvests produce more top quality pearls.

Tahitian pearls are expensive because each pearl takes a long time and a lot of care to produce and each oyster produces only one pearl.

P. margaritifera can grow quite large in the wild— sometimes up to 30cm across – and live for up to thirty years, but farmed shells are more often around 10–15cm and will be kept for between four and seven years, depending on whether the farmer does second and third grafts. It takes about eighteen months to two years for a spat to be large enough to be grafted

THE LAW

Until very recently all Tahitian pearls had to have 0.8mm of nacre around 80 per cent of the nucleus. That law was scrapped in June 2016. It was unenforceable, because there was widespread smuggling of pearls that did not meet this standard (every pearl needed to be individually x-rayed). Not only was inspection and enforcement patchy, with some substandard pearls passed and some acceptable pearls failed, but it stifled innovation. Since then farmers have responded by experimenting with a soufflé technique, and one farm is now producing pearls in the 6mm to 9mm range. The law was also problematic with regard to keishi pearls, which do not have a nucleus at all.

with a nucleus, and then the same time again before a pearl can be harvested.

In that time the oysters have to be kept clean. Most farms clean the shells manually, although one or two are successfully simply moving lines to depths where native fish will pick off seaweeds, barnacles, worms and other sea flora which congest the oysters and compete for food – it's akin to keeping down the weeds.

Selecting Tahitian Pearls

Perhaps more than any other seawater pearl, Tahitians are variable in shape, colour and size. So there is no prescriptive right pearl or wrong pearl. Choose only the pearls that you fall in love with. It really doesn't matter about the quality; they need to excite. Pick pearls that suit your skin tone and colouring, rather than an outfit, because the right pearls will enhance your complexion. But be aware of the many

A huge pile of loose, undrilled Tahitian pearls. One way to spend a few hours is to find the pairs from this.

A huge range in size is possible with Tahitian pearls. Here the big drops – probably third graft – are between 15.3mm and 17.7mm, and the tiny pearls are from the Collins Tahitian farm and measure between 7mm and 7.8mm. Collins is the only Tahitian pearl farmer growing these tiny pearls, and some of his production is only 6mm.

pitfalls, not least the fake Tahitians labelled 'Tahitian black pearls' where 'Tahitian black' is a colour of dye used on freshwater pearls; these appear all over websites such as eBay.

What size pearl do you want?

Tahitian pearls range from 5mm to 17mm. Very rarely they are larger, but probably no larger than 20mm.

Quality

Most sellers use the A–AAA grading, perhaps adding in their own named 'AAA-plus' grade, but Tahiti confusingly has its own system as well:

A grade pearls are at least 90 per cent perfect, with great lustre and no more than two imperfections within the remaining 10 per cent.
B grade pearls must have great lustre as well, but only 70 per cent of the total surface has to be without flaws.
C grade pearls must have decent lustre, with 40 per cent of the surface being clean of imper-

fections. These pearls may be used in strands for necklaces and bracelets where full drilling can tuck away many flaws.
D grade pearls are not very good.

Colour

The colour – whatever it is – should have life. It should have vibrancy, and ideally there should be blushes and overtones of more colours over a strong base colour (usually green). 'Tahitian black' fakes have colours that tend to be more homogenous so will not 'move' as the pearl moves.

When looking at a strand, it should be well balanced. Are all the colours of the strand the same intensity and depth? And if you put the two ends of the strand together, do the left and right halves balance – so that the pearls are the same size, shape and colour intensity on both sides?

Lustre

A dull pearl will look dull. But a pearl with great lustre will have enough dazzle to hide small imperfections.

Surface

Typical flaws are 'fishbites'. These are characteristic circular indentations and a symptom of Tahitian and South Sea pearls. Circle pearls occur in other types of pearl but are considered a special and often very popular type of Tahitian pearl: they have concentric rings of colour running around them in one axis. They may also have grooves marking the banding.

A drop-shaped circle Tahitian showing clear grooves and bands of colour running horizontally around the pearl.

Shape

Round

All other things being equal, round pearls will always be the most expensive. To be classed as round they must have a diameter variance of less than 2 per cent (an 8mm pearl, for example, cannot be larger than 8.2mm or smaller than 7.8mm when measured across different diameters). The pearl should be what is called an 'eight-way' roller, which means it will roll straight in any direction on a flat surface. This perfection will usually be destined to be set singly or as one of a pair of earrings.

Semi-round/roundish will look round from a distance and to the unpractised eye. Semi-rounds, carefully drilled, can often be used in a necklace or bracelet because the small deviation from round will not show.

Sizes range from 5mm to 17mm, with around 8mm to 10mm being 'average'.

Drops

Tahitian drops tend to be plump because of that internal bead, with a tear-drop shape. The cone is often hollow. It is therefore important that drops have a good nacre depth simply for strength.

Lots of drops show circling, either bands of colour or with grooves as well. Circled pearls have concentric rings etched into the form of the pearl. Some circled pearls may only have a small percentage of surface covered in these rings, while others may be etched all over. It's not known why, but circled pearls are by far the most colourful.

Baroques

Baroques can be any shape.

Tokki pearls

Tokki pearls are a recognized sub-division. These are pearls with little bumps like small half pearls stuck randomly on them.

Hollow, freeform, soufflé Tahitians

With the abandonment of the export ban on pearls with less than 0.8mm of nacre over the bead, some farmers started to experiment and

A cheerful Tahitian tokki pearl, which looks as if it has lots of little dancing feet. Disdained by many, but loved by some for its individuality and character.

one or two produced soufflé-type Tahitian pearls. These are hollow and large and tend also to have great lustre. The nucleus is a substance that swells gradually, causing the pearl sac to expand and expand. So far there have only been a few – very expensive – strands on the market.

Tahitian keishi pearls

Keishi pearls are the serendipity pearls. They form either because the oyster has somehow rejected and expelled the nucleus so the pearl sac is empty but it goes on secreting nacre and forms a pearl a bit like a deflated balloon; or as a result of some entirely incidental damage anywhere in the body of the oyster which triggers the secretion of nacre. CIBJO does not allow the latter to be classed as natural pearls although they are outside the direct farm process. Keishi pearls have a beauty all their own and tend to be very colourful and lustrous.

Tahitian keishi pearls can be up to 10mm. They are completely irregular in shape but nearly always very lustrous. This is one common shape. Larger Tahitian keishi can be a sort of hat or bowl shape.

AKOYA PEARLS

A 7mm, white, round, 45cm-long pearl necklace remains the archetypal necklace that most people think of when they think of pearls. White, round, very shiny: a single strand is the very stuff of 'Girls with Pearls'. But while it has become 'the' classic necklace, it has a short history. Before the 1930s, the traditional gift from a father to his daughter on her twenty-first birthday was a strand of pearls, and the only pearls available were expensive wild ones. Even a strand of imitation pearls was to be prized (many of grandmother's treasured pearls are imitation: discoloured, peeling and of little monetary value, they still epitomize the love of a father for a daughter).

Akoya pearls (*P. fucata martensii*) were the first to be cultured, at the turn of the twentieth century, and the method remains much the same now as it was around 100 years ago. Most of the world's akoya pearls are still produced in Japan, though there are several akoya farms located in Vietnam, one in Australia and one in China.

Akoya pearl production is constrained by the size of the oyster. Akoya oysters are small – around 8–10mm – with thin, fragile shells. Pearls are grown on round bead nuclei, usually one per oyster (although one Vietnam farm producing very small pearls implants up to four 1.3mm nuclei into one shell to produce four

Only one farm, in Vietnam, produces these tiny 1.5–2mm akoya pearls. The shells have four grafts instead of the usual one.

Some of the natural colours produced from a few pearls: blues, silver and golds, from quite deep to near white. These pearls are between 7mm and 8mm and beautifully round and clean. Since these came from the same graft technician, the conclusion is that he or she is very skilled.

LEFT: **Rainbow-nacred akoya shell draped with a long, blue akoya pearl rope. The pearls are various shades of blue and some also show a very strong pink overtone.**

1.5mm pearls). 7mm nuclei are the norm, with some second graft pearls up to around 10mm, 11mm or even 12mm (though these are increasingly scarce). Smooth, clean pearls in such large sizes will be very rare.

Akoya oysters like to live in water five to six metres deep and in temperatures of between 20 to 28 degrees Celsius. An akoya pearl should have more than 1,000 layers of conchiolin and aragonite, each of which is between 0.35 and 0.5 microns thick (one micron is a thousandth of an millimetre).

Colours

Until recently the majority of Akoya pearls in the market were round and white. At trade shows stands would have a bewildering array of hundreds of strands of near-identical white pearls with small permutations of lustre, cleanliness and size. One or two sellers at big gem shows put a few unbleached strands almost

Multicoloured akoya pearl necklace. These are all naturally occurring colours; no dye. For some unknown reason blue seems to be fading as a natural colour, so pearls harvested recently show more silvery grey than blue.

apologetically at one end of their counter, or kept them underneath and out of sight. They were very cheap back then. There would be a few golds (including some dyed gold) and a few blues.

Then around seven years ago Chinese freshwater pearl production increased sharply in quality and naturally coloured freshwater pearls started to eclipse the heavily dyed pearls that had been most of the production. People started to appreciate and seek natural-colour freshwater pearls. Trade show buyers were buying the natural-colour freshwater pearls and some started to buy the naturally coloured akoya as well. Prices more than doubled in six months as akoya sellers realized what they had was marketable after all.

Akoya pearls can come in shades of blue from pale to dark blue. They can be gold – again in shades from a light champagne to deep, rich gold. They can be grey, green, purple or violet. The extraordinary thing about this explosion of colour is that while some of it is clearly genetically present, no one is entirely certain why the blues happen (and then why whatever causes blue affects also gold genetic pearls to produce green akoya). It is probably a combination of genetics, environment and some form of contamination. Or it might be something else entirely. The odd thing is that at the time of writing blue pearls are becoming paler and scarcer while purple and violet pearls have started appearing. Scrutiny of akoya shell nacre shows that while white is predominant there is evidence that other shades are genetically present, but only in the palest of blush shades, not the dark shades of blue and purple/violet.

Most akoya pearls are still bleached, though. There are many shades of white. Most akoya are bleached to white, then often a subtle rose blush is added. This blush should only be noticeable when the pearls are laid on true white paper or next to true white pearls. At any other time they will look white. Other overtones can be blue,

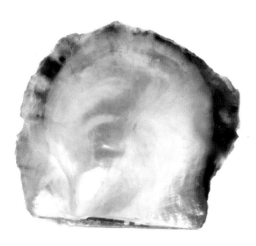

Normal and naturally coloured white and rainbow colours inside this akoya oyster shell. You can clearly see the blues and pinks that sometimes colour the pearls.

Beautiful, natural, really intense gold hidden inside this akoya shell.

green and silver. Silver overtone makes a pearl appear very white against skin.

Silver nitrate and other silver salts are used to dye akoya black, although it is increasingly difficult to find dyed black akoya pearls. The process involves soaking the pearls in weak silver nitrate and ammonia and then exposing them to light or gas, which causes the conchiolin to appear black (just like printing a photograph). The process produces a pearl that is very black: it can look more like a bead than a pearl.

Exposing an akoya to cobalt60 radiation will heighten any blue colour. In this case the effect is caused by a darkening of the freshwater nucleus rather than the akoya nacre – freshwater nacre is more susceptible to colour-changing radiation treatment.

Most of the really deep gold akoya available

are dyed. Natural-white colour is possible but unusual.

Shape

Most akoya pearls will be round or near to round, due to being grown on a round nucleus, and for a relatively short time, although some

Natural white, undyed, unpinked, round akoya. Natural white pearls as opposed to bleached pearls are a collectable for the pearl connoisseur.

will still manage to produce tails (fireballs) or be noticeably on the spectrum of off-round to baroque to drop. The pearls show the same wide variety of shapes and permutations as every other type of pearl, but they often do not reach market.

Surface flaws tend more to be folds, pleats or ripples in the nacre rather than holes or 'fish-bites'.

Lustre

The finest of the fine akoya will have a reflective surface as sharp as a top quality mirror or polished precious metal. The highest quality akoya pearls have the best lustre of any pearls.

Growing good pearls with a properly durable layer of nacre takes time. Akoya pearls that seem too cheap may have only the thinnest layer of nacre. Pearls with very thin nacre may even 'blink', which means that when rolled back and forth the pearl appears to blink – to show patches where there is no nacre and the nucleus is visible.

Hanadama and Madama Grading

In addition to the usual A–AAA gradings and any special gradings from the seller, some specialist gem laboratories offer a special grading of *hanadama*.

Hanadama (the Japanese word for spherical flower) is a minimum pearl quality standard award from The Pearl Science Laboratory, a small private company (or other similar companies). *Hanadama* pearls are not perfect pearls. While every company has different criteria, most allow some very slight blemishing,

A pearl with a *hanadama* certificate should be properly round, it should have remarkable lustre and a good depth of nacre (expect an x-ray on the certificate). The certificate will also state the exact colour of the pearl and any other special features that make the pearl special. There should be a photo of the pearl (however, one strand of pearls looks much like another, so be aware of the existence of photocopiers).

Madama pearls are natural-coloured (silver to blue) akoya pearls of equivalent quality to *hanadama*. They undergo all the same testing as hanadama, with one extra test to ensure the colouring is natural. The body colour will shift from blue to silver depending on the light, along with intense overtones and orient.

Akoya Pearl Buying Guide

1. Because there are plenty of white, round akoya pearls out there, the realistic option is to shop according to how much you can afford – with the important proviso that you deal with a specialist pearl seller, who buys hundreds of white akoya strands a year and can cut the best deal. Realistically, if you cannot afford this, consider top quality freshwater pearls, as the best white round freshwater pearls are now very close in quality to akoya but much cheaper.

2. Decide on what to prioritize. Is shape most important to you? Colour? Lustre? Clean surface? If you are prepared to compromise on one or more criteria, for example if your pearls are slightly off-round or have a few small surface flaws, the price should reflect this.

   If you want perfection in all criteria, there are several companies, not least Mikimoto itself, which will supply such pearls to you.

3. Price. Short-grown akoyas are plentiful in the market. A short-grown akoya pearl will usually look exactly the same as a good

quality one, but it will have only the thinnest coating of nacre over the nucleus and will have been in the oyster for a few short months. It is simple economics: a pearl farm, with 250 staff, can produce pearls that have been growing in the oyster for twelve to eighteen months and which have a good layer of nacre, or, in the same time, it can produce twice as many pearls with nacre half as thick.

Knowing your supplier and their reputation and knowledge is one way to avoid this. Inspection of pearls helps if the origin is unknown. It is possible to peer into a drill hole, if there is one, to see how thick the nacre is (not possible of course if the pearl is undrilled). Thin nacre is the biggest pitfall by far for a pearl novice buying akoya pearls. The internet is awash with them.

Akoya prices, more than prices for most other pearls, increase sharply once the pearls are over 7mm, because most oysters are nucleated with beads that will make a 7mm pearl after a year.

4. Lustre. Top quality akoya pearls have the best lustre of any pearls. The finest are as reflective as a mirror.

5. The more you pay, the fewer the blemishes: this is realistic, but it is sensible not to be overly obsessive about minor blemishes, which under most circumstances will not be visible.

6. More than any other pearl, an akoya pearl described as round must be round and not sort-of round or nearly round. All sorts of drops, baroques and nuggets are also possible.

7. Be aware that most of the very deep gold akoya pearls available have been dyed. There are natural gold akoya, and very beautiful they are too, but deep gold natural-colour akoya are very rare. Most gold akoya are a middle to light gold.

8. The same applies for blue akoya, which

seem to be less common over the last couple of years. Strong, quite dark blues used to be available – not often, but available. Now many of the pearls described as blue are more like a silver-grey with a slight overtone of blue. Again, be aware that deep blue pearls may be dyed.

Naturally coloured 10mm roundish silver (with a touch of pale blue) akoya with a strong pink overtone. Lots of flaws but the nacre looks thick and almost ladled on. Wound around are tiny 3mm to 4mm naturally coloured akoya misshapes. Most of them have tails. Some of the tails are so long and so sharp they have been nicknamed acupuncture pearls! (You can see one at three o'clock.)

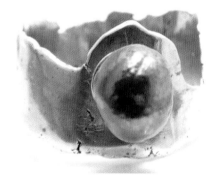

This ring, made from reclaimed and recycled silver that is not afraid to show its origin, is set with a deep blue baroque akoya pearl obtained several years ago. It's inexplicably hard to find pearls that blue now.

FRESHWATER PEARLS

Freshwater pearls are the uppity know-all adolescents of the pearl world – demanding their seat at the top table in spite of their youth. As recently as twenty years ago cultured freshwater pearls were known as 'Rice Krispies' because the only freshwater cultured pearls available resembled the breakfast cereal. They were small, oval and had indifferent lustre. They only looked good en masse in a torsade. Now the finest quality freshwater pearls rival sea-grown pearls. They have metallic lustre, flawless surface, size and a range of colours never before seen in any pearl.

Nearly all the world's cultured freshwater pearl production is in China, with a couple of niche farms in Japan. The single American farm is open as a tourist attraction but there is no pearl production any more.

Freshwater – or river or sweetwater pearls – are also outstanding for the huge variety of shapes, sizes and colours readily available, both tissue-nucleated and bead-nucleated.

Freshwater mussels can be triggered to produce pearls simply by transplanting and

The polished inside of a freshwater mussel shell. Note the 'tadpole' pearl that has grown attached to the shell. This shell has much less colour, but pinks, white and golds are still visible.

LEFT: **A freshwater mussel from China, showing all the pinks, purples, peach, blues and other shades hidden inside its genetics. The necklace and matched earrings are outstanding, naturally white, round freshwater pearls. The colour is naturally white with a faint gold blush.**

implanting a sliver of mantle tissue from a donor shell. Additionally, when tissue-only nucleating, a full-grown freshwater mussel is large enough (20mm up by around 15m and upward) to accept up to fifteen grafts on either side of the mantle, producing up to thirty pearls at a time. The molluscs are then returned to their freshwater environment, where they are tended for two to six years. The resulting pearls are of solid nacre, but without a bead nucleus to guide the growth process, the pearls are rarely round. This is why freshwater farmers have, in the last decade, developed a bead-nucleation process for freshwater mussels, which produces fewer pearls per mussel but each pearl will be of higher quality.

If in doubt as to whether a freshwater pearl is solid nacre or bead-nucleated, the 'horizon' between the bead and the mussel nacre can often be felt when drilling. A bead-nucleated pearl is more likely to be round, and some bead-nucleated pearls have a lush, glutinous thickness about the nacre as though the layers have been trowelled on instead of thinly painted. But usually the supplier will know.

Freshwater nacre is laid down much faster than saltwater pearl nacre, but even so most nucleated pearls take at least a year to grow (up to seven years between nucleation and harvest). Which explains why they are so much more expensive.

Solid nacre freshwater pearls are becoming increasingly rare. It is understandable that pearl farmers want to assure themselves that their pearls will be round and therefore of high value compared to other shapes. All-nacre pearls in larger sizes will take years to produce, with a concomitant risk of distortions in shape, lustre and surface quality. All-nacre freshwater pearls are undoubtedly more durable but the chances of perfect round shapes are much lower. Additionally, some pearl factories are processing bead-nucleated pearls intensively, so that the pearls have stunning lustre, rivalling the finest

The outside of the freshwater mussel is as drab and camouflaged as every other shell.

akoyas. But there is a suspicion that such an intense treatment regime might cause the lustre to fade after a couple of years.

Some farms and companies are developing their own strains of mussel, selecting for quality, while other farms buy in their mussels ready nucleated. This careful breeding is producing more strongly coloured natural-colour pearls. After harvest in China, pearls go from individual farms to pearl factories where they are bleached to become white pearls, or otherwise coloured or processed, drilled and sorted, and assembled into strands.

Chinese Freshwater Pearls

The first pearls produced in China came from the cockscomb pearl mussel (*Cristaria plicata*). Each shell could produce as many as fifty pearls. Production was very high in volume but the quality was generally very low. Most pearls were 'potato' pearls, baroque lumps with a flat on one side. Almost all were peach colour, many deep-dyed into every colour of the rainbow.

Then farmers started to use the triangle shell mussel (*Hyriopsis cumingii*). The triangle shell produced fewer pearls, accepting only twelve to sixteen grafts per valve for a total production of twenty-four to thirty-two pearls. Quality immediately improved and has carried on improving until now when, after nearly twenty years, flawless round pearls are available with a metallic lustre that rival top quality akoya pearls. At the same time, lower quality pearls have also improved – a flat-sided potato pearl is now unusual. Dyes have all but disappeared as well, with customers appreciating a full range of natural colours.

It is estimated that Chinese production is 95 per cent of world pearl production. Natural, undyed freshwater pearls now come in shades from such a pale gold as to be white, through

1 kilo scooped at random from a consignment of freshwater pearls sent direct from a Chinese pearl farm to a pearl factory. A few were of reasonable quality, but only two pearls from the whole kilo were round. Generally they would be graded A.

This shows how bad pearls can be. These are the really bad pearls from that same kilo.

JAPANESE BIWA AND KASUMI PEARLS

In Lake Biwa (near Kyoto) early in the twentieth century a few pearl farmers started to grow pearls using the native *Hyriopsis schlegeli*. For around fifty years this farming was very successful, although most of the pearls were not round; most resembled short twigs or baby's teeth. By the early 1970s, when production was at its peak, six tons of Biwa pearls were produced per year. Not long after this, the lake became so polluted that the mussels could no longer survive and there is now no production, although the term Biwa pearl was so firmly and widely known that it became synonymous as a descriptor of any stick-shaped pearl and is still commonly incorrectly used.

More recently, farmers have established a niche farming project in Lake Kasumigaura (the second largest lake in Japan, 60km to the north-east of Tokyo), where they are producing a small harvest by crossing the Biwa pearl mussel *Hyriopsis schlegeli* with its close relative *Hyriopsis cumingi* from China. This industry has also nearly ceased production, due to eutrophicatal pollution (too many minerals and nutrients causing dangerous algae blooms). These Kasumi pearls are distinctive for being large, with a wrinkled surface, metallic or satiny lustre and intense colouration. But they are nearly indistinguishable from the pearls grown in China from similar hybrid mussels and usually called ripple pearls (*see* below).

These are not Biwa pearls, but they are a good approximation of what they looked like, although they are perhaps too shiny, too smooth and too big to be Biwa.

golds, peach, pinks, lavender and purple, with patches or overtones in every shade plus blues and greens (and some pearls even show patches of distinct red).

'Soufflé' pearls

Even larger pearls are being produced with pearls nucleated with a compound that expands as it absorbs water and thereby stretches the pearl sac. These pearls, third graft, often have stunning lustre and an undulating surface. When drilled, the compound is cleaned out.

The pearls are called soufflé pearls because they are hollow and lightweight for their size, and because they are hollow they present special difficulties in setting and stringing. They can be spectacular; however, they had all but disappeared by 2020.

Edison/Ming/ripple/bead-nucleated tadpoles

Around twelve years ago there was a flood of odd pearls onto the market. They looked like tadpoles, with a head and a tail often over 1cm long. The nacre looked as if it had been poured on thickly.

Then a short while later, a few 12mm to 14mm single pearls appeared, in all-natural colours, as did at the same time a few (the main dealer had six strands) remarkable pearls – up to 15mm, roundish, very colourful in natural shades and with a never-before-seen but attractive wrinkly skin. These were the first bead-nucleated pearls. (There had been bead-nucleated pearls before – coin-shaped discs or heart shapes, for example – but they were not thought of as specifically bead-nucleated. They were shaped pearls with a bead.)

Edison is the brand name given to a range of

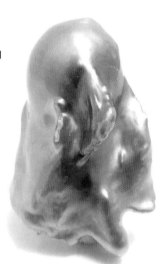

A great example of a bead-nucleated fireball pearl. You can see the large bead forming the head and the tail is formed of luxurious swathes of nacre. These pearls are shaped when the development of the pearl sac goes wrong, but they can be incredibly dramatic.

large, bead-nucleated freshwater pearls from one leading Chinese supplier. One early strand of these pearls achieved £0.5m at auction. The pearls come from the same *Hyriopsis* hybrid between *Hyriopsis cumingi* and *Hyriopsis schlegeli* that produces Kasumi pearls. Edison pearls at their finest will show intense metallic lustre, a clean surface and a range of natural colours from white to a deep purple, as well as shades of pinks, lavenders, peaches and golds. Some pearls even show green or blue. Sizes range from around 10mm to 20mm.

Ming pearls are what non-Edison pearls are called. Ming is a generic term applied to the bead-nucleated pearls that don't come from the producer of Edison pearls (which is a brand). They are approaching Edison pearls in quality, but are perhaps a year behind.

Ripple pearls are bead-nucleated pearls with a distinctive wrinkled surface, often a mix of satin and metallic lustre, a stunning shimmering play of colours, and often an effect like gold leaf added in patches.

Freshwater Treatments

Grey: silver nitrate and gamma radiation. Most pearls treated to grey will be a mid-grey with average lustre, while one or two in a hundred will turn super-lustrous and either pink/grey or blue/grey.

Black: dyed. A good dye process will bring out a range of colours and even peacock effects. Over-dying will produce a heavy black mono-chrome. Beware of 'Tahitian black' colour pearls, which are freshwater pearls dyed to imitate Tahitian pearls. 'Tahitian black' pearls are common on auction sites.

Gold: bead-nucleated pearl producers are trying to emulate the deep gold of South Sea pearls to produce huge, valuable pearls at great prices. They are close, but mostly the colour isn't quite right yet. Be suspicious if the pearls are too cheap for what they appear to be.

Bright, deep colours: various dyes can be used to colour pearls the same as fabrics. This was common practice twenty years ago as a way of making very low quality potato pearls commercially viable, but it is now quite difficult to find bright, deeply coloured, dyed pearls.

Buying Freshwater Pearls

As always, if something pearl-related is too good to be true, it probably is. There are a lot of people selling freshwater pearls who claim to be selling the best, or claim to be selling 1 per cent of the harvest, or claim to be selling round pearls that aren't.

Be aware that Chinese ripple pearls are virtu-ally indistinguishable from Kasumi pearls, but cost 10 per cent of the price. Ming pearls are not particularly special, nor are they a brand.

A 'ripple' bead-nucleated pearl, so called because of its rippled surface. Lustre tends to be superb and the best ripple pearls have stupendous colours. This pearl is 18.5mm by 17.3mm.

There is nothing wrong with buying some of the dyed gold South Sea-ish imitation pearls, as long as you don't re-sell them as South Sea pearls. Unlike sea pearls, every shape, size and colour variation of freshwater pearls is readily available.

A strand of freshwater 'rosebud' or granulated pearls – these are potato pearls with unusual surfaces, which range between granulated and satin, mixed in with patches of high lustre. Unusual and attractive, but hard to find because most sellers think they are rejects.

OTHER PEARLS

A pearl that is 'wild' (i.e. one which has grown without any human activity or intervention) is called a natural pearl. Natural pearls are very rare these days and so command high prices.

British Natural Pearls

Margaritifera margaritifera

Found in many European Union countries and in parts of the USA and Canada.

Margaritifera is a remarkable organism. It has negligible senescence (It doesn't get old) and it is thought, though without full confirmation as yet, that the maximum lifespan may be 210–250 years.

It also has an extraordinarily complex life cycle. In early summer each year, male mussels release sperm into the water and they are inhaled by female mussels. Inside the female, the fertilized eggs develop in a pouch on the gills for several weeks, until temperature or other environmental cues trigger the female to release the larvae back into the water. A mature female will eject around one to four million larvae (size between 0.6mm and 0.7mm) over a couple of days. These tiny, fully formed mussels are inhaled by a salmon or trout and then as the fish exhales them the larvae snap

THE LAW

Freshwater pearl mussels are a strictly protected species across Europe. In the UK the relevant law is Schedule 5 of the Wildlife and Countryside Act 1981 (as amended) and Annex 2 of the Habitats Directive. You're breaking the law if you:

- capture, kill, disturb or injure them (on purpose or by not taking enough care)
- damage or destroy their breeding or resting places (even accidentally)
- obstruct access to their resting or sheltering places (on purpose or by not taking enough care)
- possess or sell freshwater mussel pearls (this does include on eBay) harvested after 1998

If you're found guilty of an offence you could get an unlimited fine and up to six months in prison. And you can't do anything that might affect the water in which there even *might* be mussels: in northern England, Shropshire and Devon, the Mawddach and Wye river catchments in Wales, and twenty-one rivers in Scotland.

LEFT: **Pipi pearls will always only ever be tiny – but what little golden rays of sunshine they are! This necklace is made of 1,700 pipis from the Cook Islands: 3–3.5mm, collected in the 1970s, on twelve strands, with an 18k handmade clasp and with interspersed peridot, garnet, amethyst and amber. It has a name: Te Poe Pipi O Te Kuki Airani. (Photo: Steve Metzler)**

their shells closed onto the fish's gills. They'll stay there, hitching a ride, until the following May/June when they will drop off and snuggle down in the gravel of fast-moving, clean and well-oxygenated water.

The total UK population is around half a million adult mussels – most in Scotland but also, for example, an estimated 30,000 in the North Tyne area (northeast England), where there is an active scheme to rejuvenate stocks by attaching bred larvae to trout to be released into the River Tyne.

The shells grow very slowly. At seven years they will be less then 3cm long, most of which will be buried under the riverbed. It will be around another decade before these mussels will be old enough to breed.

The earliest reference in Britain to freshwater mussels is by Julius Caesar's biographer, Suetonius, who stated that Caesar's admiration of pearls was a reason for the first Roman invasion in 55 BC.

Wild Pearls around the World

These pearls can mostly be drilled to set them, but they can be both very hard and very brittle,

---

ORMER LAW

In the UK's Channel Islands *Haliotis tuberculata*, the ormer, can only be collected from 1 January to 30 April, at full or new moon and two days following that. No ormers may be taken from the beach which are under 80mm in shell length (90mm in Jersey). Anyone gathering them may not wear a wetsuit and may not put their head under water. The law is enforced – the world's first underwater arrest occurred when a man from Guernsey was illegally diving for ormers and was arrested by a police officer in full diving gear.

---

especially conch and clam, so be prepared for cracks and breakages. Drilling will also diminish the notional value.

Abalone

Haliotis. Over 100 subspecies widely distributed around the world.

Abalone pearls are very rare – most often they are horn-shaped, fragile and unstable. A round abalone pearl is exceptionally rare, espe-

There are many species of abalone around the world. Their shells are almost all beautiful.

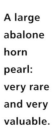

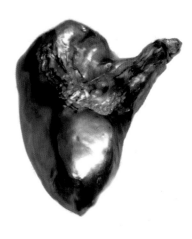

A large abalone horn pearl: very rare and very valuable.

cially over 2mm. They range in size between 7 and 30cm and are prized for the spectacular mother of pearl on the inside of their shells, which is often whorled and highly coloured as well as very lustrous. Colours range between silvery white, pink, green-red, deep blue, green or purple. The shells are very strong and resilient; their structure is being studied by materials scientists looking to strengthen ceramics.

Abalone are edible and are farmed for their meat. Wild abalone stocks are diminishing and most areas now offer legal protection.

In New Zealand one farm has pioneered raising blue paua *Haliotis iris* abalone mabé pearls. This New Zealand native abalone produces a distinctive and stunningly iridescent blue pearl but is very hard to nucleate as its blood does not clot, so any damage will kill it. Mabé are produced.

Bahrain or Basra pearls

Pinctada radiata (Gulf pearl oyster), and to a lesser extent *Pinctada margaritifera* (black-lipped pearl oyster).

Natural or wild pearls from the Persian Gulf are probably the most rare and valuable pearls in the world today. They have been prized for millennia: an Assyrian inscription from around 2000 BC talks of fish eyes from Dilmun, an ancient civilization of which Bahrain was capital. Pliny said that Tylos, the classical name for Bahrain, was famous for the vast number of its pearls. The apogee of the trade was between around 1850 and 1930. Pearls were the most valuable gemstone known to man, worth far more than diamonds. About 30,000 divers merely held their breath (scuba was not invented until 1943). Their only equipment was a nose peg, leather finger stalls to protect against coral, a weighted rope and a bag.

A combination of the world Depression and the development of farming by Mikimoto destroyed demand. Some oyster beds survive and you can day-dive to collect your own unique souvenir.

It is illegal to import cultured pearls into Bahrain, so protective are they of their pearl trade. Traditionally, the pearls were displayed on red cloth and the two parties negotiated by a sort of touch language with their hands draped in a red cloth to hide the discussion from third party rival eyes!

Blue mussel

Mytilus edulis. Worldwide distribution.

These mussels commonly produce very small pearls, of the order of 0.5mm to 1mm. Any pearl over this size is unusual. Various colours, often with a waxy lustre. Edible.

Cassis

Cassis Cornuta or helmet shell. Found in the Red Sea, the Indian Ocean, off the southern African coast from northern KwaZulu-Natal and from Mozambique, as well as in the Pacific Ocean. It is especially welcome in Queensland, Australia because it eats the Crown of Thorns starfish.

Pearls are pale orange, and sometimes round.

Clams

Tridacna gigas (giant clam). Found in the South Seas.

Giant clam can be huge – up to a metre and weighing 250kg. The Pearl of Allah regularly pops up in newspapers as an example of a huge pearl (24cm, 6.4kg). It is very ugly indeed. Various inflated prices are usually quoted based on the multiplied weight of gem quality pearls.

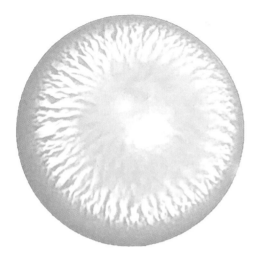

A specimen white clam pearl with clear flame.

Not much flame, but a matched pair of conch pearls is a remarkable find.

Conch pearls come in many colours from near white to brown, via orange. The most valuable are a deep salmony pink with orange close behind. A small, deep pink, flawless and regularly shaped conch pearl will be worth considerably more than a much larger, irregular, two-colour pearl.

Tridacna squamosa

The most beautiful – and most valuable – clam pearls are pure white and round. The elusive but coveted flame effects, made of prisms of aragonite, with a fine silk-like sheen, can often only be seen in reflected light.

Mercenaria mercenaria (quahog clam). Found on the east American coast from Canada to Georgia, especially on the coast of New England states.

Quahog pearls come in white, reddish-brown, pink, purple or blackish and are very hard and porcellaneous with gloss, and the surface may show a flame structure with a silk effect or a strange honeycomb structure made up of tiny irregularities.

Melo melo

Melo melo (common name: the Indian volute or bailer shell). Found in Southeast Asia, from Burma, Thailand and Malaysia, to the South China Sea and the Philippines.

A known carnivore, this snail-like shelled mollusc preys on other molluscs. Melo is quite large – between 15cm and 17cm – with an ochre yellow shell blotched with brown.

The pearls are a by-product of fishing for this large, edible mollusc. The shell is also useful as a scoop because its mouth is large.

Conch

Mostly *Strombus gigas*.

Rarest of the natural pearls, conch (pronounced conk) pearls look a bit like jelly beans. They are not nacreous but have a distinctive flame pattern on the surface. The colours range from orange, through yellow to pink.

Gold and white melo melo pearl: swirls rather than flame.

The shell of the penguin is distinctively shaped. They are cultured for mabé but there are natural pearls to be found as well.

Pteria species

Pteria penguin. Found from the East African coast and the Red Sea to India, southern China, southern Japan, the Philippines, Indonesia and northern Australia.

Penguin pearls are a deep bronzy brown, echoing the shells from which they come. Penguin are cultured for mabé in the Ryukyu Islands, along the southern coast of China, on Phuket Island in Thailand, and on Vava'u in Tonga.

Sea of Cortez pearls/ Pacific wing-oyster

Pteria sterna. Found in the Gulf of California and Mexico.

Pteria sterna, commonly known as the rainbow-lipped pearl oyster, is found in the Gulf of California. One farm in Mexico cultures them (see below). These native pearls were fished almost to extinction before being conserved and stocks developed by the founding of one pearl farm. This farm, in the Sea of Cortez, Mexico, produces very rare pearls from *Pteria sterna*, the rainbow-lipped oyster (the indigenous pearl oyster). These pearls fluoresce red under UV light due to their unique metal-proteins called porphyrins. The pearl colour default is a light silvery grey but, true to their name, Cortez pearls can show a rainbow of colour, including a strong mid-blue. The farm has been operating since 2004 so the total number of these pearls is very small and the price correspondingly very high. The farm produces both free pearls and mabés.

The Pacific wing-oyster naturally produces grey, pink, golden, green and purplish pearls. Grafting is complex because the oysters are small, the shells are thin and the shape of the shell makes the seeding operation difficult; the pearl sack is wide at the base, which means that the graft may shift around.

The farm uses both farm-raised and wild spat.

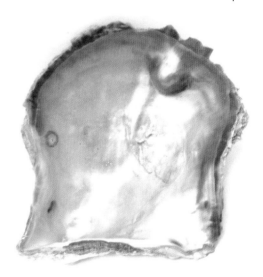

Pteria sterna shells are quite small, so implanting a nucleus is a delicate procedure. The one farm cultivating them is protecting the environment so that wild stocks, fished almost to extinction by unregulated pearl hunters, are recovering. The farm produces round pearls and mabé.

Pipi

Pinctada maculata. Found in Polynesia and the Cook Islands.

As if Polynesia wasn't blessed enough by having *Pinctada maculata*, the black-lipped oyster, the archipelago also has these tiny gems. They are called pipi (Tahitian for small or tiny) pearls and are mostly found on Penryhn (also known as Tongareva), one of the most remote of the remote Cook Islands. They are the smallest of the oceanic pearls producing oysters and possibly the direct ancestor of all of them. They produce bright, lustrous, deep-golden pearls but which are too small to be farmed on a realistic commercial basis. The shells are only about 20mm and the pearls range from 2mm to 5mm.

Scallop

Pectinidae species. Widespread distribution.

These pearls are unusual, and can be anything from white to speckled, resembling a very small bird's egg. Edible. More advanced biologically than other pearl shells, scallops have up to 200 rudimentary but bright blue eyes.

Scallop shells are probably the archetypal shell shape (remember Tony Curtis's line in *Some Like It Hot:* 'My father and my grandfather had a passion for shells, that's why we named the oil company after it').

Scallops are edible and are widely available. Very occasionally they produce a pearl.

CIBJO

The World Jewellery Confederation, founded in 1961, is the ultimate arbiter on matters to do with anything relating to jewellery. Resistant to change and slow to innovate, it insists that every cultured pearl be clearly identified as such (which would make websites extremely tedious) and that every keishi pearl is cultured because the oyster has been farmed, even when the specific pearl is clearly formed outside of anything to do with any culturing process. This is mostly a question of provenance and value because wild pearls are always more costly and sought after.

For further information about pearls, contact the author at Wendy@Pearlsapractical.guide.

INDEX

AA-AAA 9,10–11, 31
   Tahitian 73
abalone 90
akoya 77–81
aragonite 8, 9, 10, 78

bailer shell 92
bamboo tweezers 17, 71
baroque 13
bead nucleated 10
biwa 15, 85
bleaching 24
blue mussel 91
brooch bars 49
British natural pearls 89
   legal protection 89
buttons 12
buying pearls 29–32, 66, 80, 87

care 16–17
charity shops 31
Christaria plicata 8
CIBJO 94
claws/prongs 48
classification 9, 10, 73
coins 15
colours
   akoya 78
   south sea 63
   Tahitian 70, 73
   freshwater 77
conch 92
conchiolin 8, 9, 78
Cortez, Sea of 93
cultured 9

designer makers 30
drilling pearls 39 –43
drops/drips 12, 74

Edison 10, 86
elliptical/rice 12

factory 22
fake pearls 32
farmed 9
farming 19–22
   akoya pearls 77
   freshwater pearls 83
   South Sea pearls 62
   Tahitian pearls 71
findings 49
fireballs 12
French wire 52–53
freshwater pearls 83 – 87
full drilled pearls 48

gas pearl 16
gender 7
gem shows 30
general biology 7
giant clam 91
global warming 27
glueing 46
grading
   akoya 80
gulf pearl 91
Gulf of Mexico pearls 93

half drilled pearls 36, 45
Haliotis species 90
Haliotis tuberculata 90
Hanadama 80
harvest 22
holiday souvenirs 30
hollow pearls 57
Hong Kong show 26
Hyriopsis cuming 10
Hyriopsis Schegal 10

internet platforms   29

kasumi   85
keishi   14, 65, 66, 75
kilo weight   25,36
knotting pearls   51–59

leather   58–59,
loose nucleus   57
lustre   80
   akoya   80

Madama   80
maeshori   24
Margaritifera margaritifera   89
mantle tissue   7, 21, 22
measuring pearls   25
Melo melo   92
Mercenaria mercenaria   92
Mikimoto   34
ming   86
multiple peg settings   45
mytilus edulls   91

nacre   8–9
nacre depth law   72
natural   9
nugget   13

ormer   90

pearl care   16
pearl grading   10
shapes   11
pectinidae species   94
Pinctada fucata martensii   77
Pinctada maculata   94
Pinctada margaritifera   69
Pinctada maxima   61 –67
Pinctada Radiata   91
pipi pearls   94
pinking   78
porphyrins   9
prongs   48
potato   15
Pteria penguin   93
Pteria sterna   93

quahog   92

rainbow-lipped oyster   93
real or fake?   32
rice   12
ripple   15, 86
Rome   14
round   11, 74

scallop   94
selection   25, 35, 37
selling pearls   25
semi round   12
setting pearls   45 –49
shops   29
soufflé   16, 74, 86
South Sea pearls   63–67
specialist sellers   30
sticks   14
strands   36
stringing materials   53
Strombus gigas   92
superglue   46

Tahitian pearls   69–75
three pin setting   45–46
three strand necklaces   58
tokki   16
treatments   23, 71, 78–9,   87
Tridacna gigas   91
Tridacna Squamosa   92
Tucson show   26

undrilled pearls   36, 48
unglueing   47

volute shell   92

water   9
wholesalers   35, 36
wire wrapping   48